T0208691

Amazon Girl

Dare to Dream

Elizabeth Demarest

WESTBOW
PRESS

A DIVISION OF THOMAS NELSON
& ZONDERVAN

WestBow Press books may be ordered through booksellers or by contacting:

WestBow Press
A Division of Thomas Nelson & Zondervan
1663 Liberty Drive
Bloomington, IN 47403
www.westbowpress.com
1 (866) 928-1240

Because of the dynamic nature of the Internet, any web addresses or
links contained in this book may have changed since publication and
may no longer be valid. The views expressed in this work are solely those
of the author and do not necessarily reflect the views of the publisher,
and the publisher hereby disclaims any responsibility for them.

Any people depicted in stock imagery provided by Thinkstock are models,
and such images are being used for illustrative purposes only.
Certain stock imagery © Thinkstock.

ISBN: 978-1-4908-4781-8 (sc)
ISBN: 978-1-4908-4782-5 (e)

Library of Congress Control Number: 2014914457

Printed in the United States of America.

WestBow Press rev. date: 12/11/2014

After years of encouragement to share her amazing story, Elizabeth Demarest finally has done so—and it's a bombshell. I love, love, love the heartbeat of this awesome book! The love Jesus has for us leaps off the pages. You feel like you're right next to Elizabeth, whether she's canoeing on the Amazon or cowering under the covers. I dare you to read this book. It will touch a nerve. It will seize your heart. It will make you fall in love with Jesus all over again.

Christine Caine, Founder
The A21 Campaign

Contents

Acknowledgments

First, all praise and glory to God for giving me dreams and keeping them alive. Throughout the process of writing this book, many individuals helped to make this dream a reality. Special thanks go to Joy Holden and Jason Forbus. Joy listened to me as I shared my story for the first time, and believed we could do this together, not to mention she loves Brazil. She invested her time and talent in editing as well as working with me creatively to craft my story. Jason then spent countless hours editing and bringing this project to the finish line. I thought he was a workaholic, but it turns out he just wanted to finish before the 2014 FIFA World Cup! Thank you both for your sacrifice and support.

I want to dedicate this book to my three munchkins. I know they are too little to read it yet, but one day they will. My dream for you—Nathanael, Benjamin, and Gisele—is that you will also take risks and embrace all that God has for you. Life is filled with great adventures, so don't miss out! Although he would rather not be mentioned, this book would not be possible without my husband, Aley, who constantly encouraged me over the years. He's my perfect match!

Finally, thank you. Yes, you—the one reading this. Thank you for taking the time to hear my story. I would love to hear from you. You can reach me at AmazonGirlBook@gmail.com.

Introduction

Hope deferred makes the heart sick, but a
dream fulfilled is a tree of life.

—Proverbs 13:12 NLT

I couldn't look. I couldn't move. I couldn't breathe. The humidity choked me. A macaw screamed at me. Jabbering monkeys surrounded me. My brothers' shouts pierced the jungle: "Elizabeth! Just jump already!" I forced my eyes open to a wobbly world of deep green. Flecks of sunlight danced from the canopy above to the water below—far, far below. My toes kept me anchored to the tree limb, but my sweaty hands kept slipping on the buttery vine. I flapped around like a human sail. The macaw seemed to scream louder. The monkeys seemed to edge closer. *Just jump already!* I stole a quick breath, wrapped the rubbery vine around my arm, and stepped off my limb of safety. I whooped triumphantly as I soared through the trees. At just the right moment, I let go and splashed into the cool water.

Like city kids, my four brothers and I often pretended to swing from tree to tree like Tarzan. Unlike city kids, we didn't have a jungle gym; the jungle *was* our gym. A missionary child, I grew up in the wild and dangerous Amazon Rainforest of Brazil.

Unlike Tarzan, who wound up in a tropical world by tragic happenstance, my parents chose this environment as their home. My mother is a native Brazilian, and my father is an American that grew up in the Amazon as a missionary child—just like me. I enjoy dual citizenship (Brazilian by birth, American because my father is), but I'm an Amazon girl through and through.

Although growing up in the jungle was amazing, my life with Christ far exceeds it. God gave me specific dreams for my life that, years later, became reality. Though some think that following Christ is a boring religious activity, a forced weekly ritual to impress God, my spiritual journey, like my life in the jungle, is far from boring.

Aside from my relationship with Christ, which is the most important part of my life, His church has been my constant anchor. Throughout my life, whether in the Amazon or in America, the local church has been the vehicle that brought me to my destiny and sustained me to live out my dreams. Guess what? The local church can be the same for you!

In this book, I share my adventures, my struggles, my hurt as a young girl, and the fulfillment of my dreams. Though I may describe joyful experiences, painful interruptions, and fear of the unknown, I hope each chapter inspires you to never give up on your dreams. I encourage you to hang onto your faith and find the courage to step off your limb of safety and soar into the great adventure that God has for you. With God, nothing is impossible. God is the dream giver, and He's deposited dreams inside you that He's just waiting to fulfill. Take this journey with me, and witness how my dreams—which were really God's dreams for me—came true.

Amazon Girl's Dreams

A fternoon coffee was a tradition in my grandparents' home. Every day, after a little siesta, Grandpa made coffee the old-fashioned way: on the stovetop. He added coffee powder into a cotton strainer, brought water to a boil, and let it soak. After I poured the syrupy coffee into a cup, I added lots of sugar and powdered milk. I grabbed my cup and some bread (made daily in the bakery down the street) and went to my Grandma Socorro.

We sat in a swing on her front porch, facing the busy street as we faced my future and dreamed of all the possibilities before me. She often asked the question that adults have asked children for generations: *What do you want to do when you grow up?* No matter what I said, Grandma always supported me and never discouraged me. One day, however, the ordinarily whimsical conversation took a serious turn. Grandma gave me a piece of paper and asked me to write my dreams down so she could pray for them every day. Wow. This felt grown-up and serious. Before I share those dreams that Grandma and I wrote down nearly two decades ago, you need to know her story.

Grandma Socorro grew up in the small town of Boca do Acre, Brazil. When her mother died, Grandma became the female leader of the home—at four years old. Home responsibilities plus extreme distance forced her to quit school around third grade. Let me explain what I mean by extreme distance. Maybe I should say difficult travel. Grandma and her cousin traveled thirty minutes to school—and thirty minutes home—every day. In a canoe. On the Amazon River. By themselves. At ages six and seven. The realities of life on the Amazon conspired against Grandma's formal education.

At sixteen, Grandma Socorro married Grandpa Antonio. They moved to the big city of Manaus, the capital of the Amazon, and started a family. The birth of one child followed another. Then another. And another. The grand total? Fifteen. Working in the boat industry, Grandpa had to travel a lot—while Grandma stayed in the city with the children. My mother was one of the oldest, so she helped raise her younger siblings.

Grandma was a woman of faith. She believed the Bible was true. Grandma believed that no dream was too big or impossible. By the time I was born, she had been walking with Jesus for years, always grateful that her dad, my great-grandfather, had introduced her to Christ.

Now you know Grandma a little better, so let's go back to our afternoons on the front porch.

Exchanging jungle life for a trip to the big city to visit my grandparents was always a highlight for me. Of course, Grandma cooked amazing food and nurtured us, but her number one goal and passion was to teach us what it meant to walk with Jesus. I can still picture her cradling her tattered Bible, clutching it close to her heart as she prayed. She faithfully read it every morning and afternoon. Her relationship with God was sacred, intimate.

Over the years, she instilled in me that nothing was impossible with God; she knew that this ancient God of the Bible was true to His Word. Her close walk with Yahweh gently guided me to be a believer who dared to dream the impossible—and never give up on those dreams. So, with childlike faith, I wrote down seven dreams, in checklist format, and handed the list to Grandma as we sat on her porch.

Here is that list:

- *um marido*
- *um emprego*
- *um carro*
- *vitória*
- *sabedoria*
- *inteligência*
- *escrever um livro*

Um marido. A husband was first on my list. Grandma, wanting me to choose wisely, imparted to me the seriousness of marrying the right man. She and her husband, my mother's parents, are both still alive and recently celebrated sixty years of marriage. My dream was to have a lifelong love like theirs.

I scratched off *um emprego e um carro* (a job and a car). Maybe I thought I could make those happen with my own ability, so I scratched them off.

Vitória. Victory was next. I wanted to be a winner in everything I put my hands to. I did not want to lose in life.

Sabedoria. Wisdom followed victory. Oh, how I would need this one. Observing Grandma and her lifestyle of wisdom made me long for the same.

Inteligência. Intelligence was my next dream. As English was my second language, school was a struggle.

Finally, my last dream: *escrever um livro* (to write a book). This last one is my favorite. You're reading a dream that came true.

> For nothing is impossible with God.
> —Luke 1:37 NIV

An angel proclaimed this to Mary, the mother of Jesus, while delivering a promise about her future, a future that changed the course of human history. In that moment, Mary was given a seed of greatness, a dream that was impossible in the natural. Mary, a young teenager, was given the honor to carry Jesus *in utero.* She had a choice: believe the dream or abort it.

Choosing to believe is the hard part. Belief and faith are so closely related that they nearly intertwine. Mary had to *choose to believe* that nothing is impossible with God. Belief is a choice, and faith is a seed, a gift. When you believe the truth with confidence to take action, you exercise faith.

Belief is an opinion or judgment in which a person is fully persuaded. When I was a child, I chose to believe that monsters lurked under my bed. I chose to believe that hairy hands and arms grabbed my legs and pulled me underneath the bed as I screamed bloody murder for someone to rescue me. It was just my imagination, but I believed it could happen. I chose to believe a lie rather than the truth. As I matured, so did my belief system. I learned to focus my imagination on faith and truth rather than fear and lies. We believe what we feed our minds. I learned to choose to believe and feed my mind with the truth of God's Word.

Take the truth from the Bible, choose to believe what it says with confidence, and take action by exercising faith. Let's use Ephesians 3:20: "Now to Him who is able to do immeasurably more than all we ask or imagine, according to his power that is at work within us." Take that verse and apply it to your life. Choose to believe that because of His power that is at work within us, God is able to do immeasurably more than all we ask or imagine.

Grandma challenged me to believe the impossible. Though her schooling ended at third grade, she taught herself to read and apply the Word of God.

If I can dream dreams and see them come true, so can you. Maybe you weren't encouraged as a young child to dream. Start today. Write down what you have always wanted to do. Whether your dream began twenty years or twenty seconds ago, write it down. Choose to believe. If I can, so can you.

Dreams through the Generations

R isk is in my DNA. My parents—and both sets of grandparents—chose risk over security because of their faith and their God-given dreams. I know how hard it is to leave family members behind, quit jobs, and move far away from home: it's part of my heritage. My forebears walked away from comfortable lives in America and gave up the privileges that a first-world country offers. They chose risk because they knew that a life of faith sometimes takes you into paths seen only by God, confident that the Holy Spirit guides with purpose and mission.

You are the link between your heritage and your legacy. If you're like me, your heritage can be intimidating—especially if your family tree is filled with high achievers whose lives seem more glamorous than yours. It's easy to fall into the trap of comparison and feel... *inferior.* Or maybe you've had a different experience. Perhaps your family tree is filled with cautionary tales and mistakes you don't want to repeat. It's easy to fall into that same trap of comparison and feel...

superior. The good news is that God is the master at using all that makes you unique—your past, your family dynamics, and your personality—to produce the beautiful and amazing person that you are. Ephesians 2:10 NLT reads, "For we are God's masterpiece. He has created us anew in Christ Jesus, so we can do the good things he planned for us long ago." You are not a mistake or an afterthought. You don't have to wish your life was like someone else's or live in regret thinking you should have been born in a different era or family. Jeremiah 29:11 NIV reads, "'For I know the plans I have for you,' declares the Lord, 'plans to prosper you and not to harm you, plans to give you hope and a future.'" You need not long for anyone else's life. God uniquely created yours. And He is greater and more powerful than any family history. A legacy of faith and hope can begin with you!

Family is a beautiful tool the Father uses to shape our destiny. He takes what our parents and grandparents have (or have not) been as individuals and uses them as building blocks in our own lives. Whether you come from an intact, loving, supportive family or a dysfunctional, abusive, broken family, He uses our families to mold us into vessels that are greater than the sum of their parts.

Our family mission started in 1948 with newlyweds obedient to God's call. Married only a year, Jennings and Sarah Williams, my father's parents, packed up their humble belongings and left the California coast to minister to an indigenous tribe in the jungles of the great Amazon Basin. I can only imagine their excitement and anxiety as they stepped off their safe world onto a ship and sailed for the unknown. Good-bye *terra firma,* hello *terra incognita.*

I wonder if they realized that they were beginning not merely their own story, but a legacy of missions that would extend to their eleven children and numerous grandchildren. Jennings and Sarah were the link between their heritage and their legacy. And what a legacy! Of those eleven children (one died tragically of diphtheria at age six), several followed a similar road of service to God and people—especially the people of Brazil. Jennings and Sarah spent nearly twenty-eight years on the mission field and earned the reputation of being passionate Jesus followers, consumed with a desire to share the good news of Christ with every life they touched. My grandparents lived out their dreams courageously.

My grandmother Sarah sets the standard for selfless determination. As a midwife, she helped deliver over a thousand babies in the Amazon basin. She unconditionally loved the children she helped deliver and often provided care for them after they arrived. In one instance, she nursed a baby for two weeks. One particular tribe, the Tapirape, had a horrifying ritual: if the mother died at childbirth, the infant was buried alive with the deceased mother! There was one occasion when, after *so many* babies were buried alive over a short period of time, the village chief spared one particular infant—a girl—whom my grandmother volunteered to nurse as her own. After two weeks, she returned the baby to the tribe, and she continued to visit her through the years. I love this picture of my grandmother providing sustenance and life to a child who was helpless and doomed without her. What an amazing example of God's love for us. Grandma Sarah grew from a surrendered young woman to a powerful woman of godly influence during her sojourn in the Amazon. Although she had no desire to leave the people she so dearly loved, God had other plans.

At the age of fifty-three, Grandma Sarah felt weak while planting some seeds, a common chore. She noticed she was hemorrhaging. Thirty days later, she was *still* hemorrhaging and finally went to the doctor. She went alone into the city, leaving her husband and family to continue their lives as usual. The doctors immediately performed an emergency hysterectomy. Sarah lost a dangerous amount of blood, and the under-equipped hospital did not have a blood bank or a blood donor to help her recover. She languished in the hospital for days.

Her lack of strength and health, however, did not prevent Grandma Sarah from sharing Christ's love with the other female patients in her room. She constantly read to them and told them they mattered to God—until the nurses tired of her convalescent evangelism and moved her to a private room.

My grandfather Jennings, concerned for his wife, sent their eleven-year-old daughter, Debbie, to keep her mother company as she recovered. Just as her mother did, Debbie traveled alone to the city. In order to see her mother outside of visiting hours, eleven-year-old Debbie volunteered at the hospital. She cared for newborns when she wasn't with her mother, leaving only to sleep at a friend's house each night. One day, my grandmother was in a great deal of pain. As Aunt Debbie leaned in to comfort her, her mother shared,

"Jesus appeared to me, and I'll go to be with Him today." Aunt Debbie cried out and begged her not to go, but Grandma Sarah knew her Lord was calling her home. The nurses heard the commotion and—misunderstanding the situation—made Aunt Debbie leave the hospital, forcing her to leave her mother who was dying. I cannot imagine the anxiety and devastation that my aunt felt that day. Debbie trudged back to the house where she was staying and sat alone on the steps—distraught, crying. Grandfather finally arrived late that afternoon, but he and his daughter missed their moment to say good-bye. Once they reached Sarah, she was unconscious. My grandma Sarah Williams indeed went to see Jesus that same day: October 16, 1976.

Sarah Williams impacted her world in death as well as in life. People came from all over the community to celebrate her life and mourn her death. My aunt remembers that nearly the entire town came to honor her as lines of mourners snaked through the streets, waiting patiently to show respect and love for such a generous woman. Once again, I treasure this image as a picture of a life devoted to Christ and to people. Though I never met her, she inspires me today through stories of her boldness and sacrifice. I sometimes wish she were with us so that I could hear more of her amazing life. What an adventure she must have had, taking care of ten kids, delivering countless babies, and traveling with my grandpa through the jungles on their missionary journeys. Together they began a legacy of faith and sacrifice that has lasted for generations.

While my grandparents were serving in Brazil, my father James enlisted in the US Air Force at the age of eighteen. The military provided a stable income that my father could send back to Brazil to help provide for his family. In the early 1970s, he was the sole provider for his parents and siblings. Once he completed his commitment to the US military, he traveled back to Brazil to be with his family in Lago de Carapanatuba. Whenever the family reached the end of their money, my dad and his brothers would travel to the nearest city to exchange their dollars for Brazilian currency. One of these routine trips changed my father's life. My father and two of his brothers hitchhiked to Manaus, the capitol of the Amazon. As usual, they stayed with an attorney friend who aided in the currency exchange. This friend, to whom I will be forever grateful, invited my father to his church.

Meanwhile, a beautiful young Brazilian woman, my mother Celia, was performing her duties at that same church as the Sunday school secretary. She walked from room to room, taking attendance and recording the offering, just like any other Sunday. She conveniently lived across the street, and after performing her duties, she went home to wait for the main service to start. When she heard singing, she grabbed her Bible, notebook, and veil and rushed out the door. As she stepped inside the small sanctuary, she quickly put on her covering. (The veil was common in those days. My mother's veil was made of beautiful white lace with scalloped details on the hem.) As she scanned the room for a seat, a powerful urge drew her eyes to the front row. My mother explains it as if someone gently tapped her shoulder and whispered, "Look up to the front row to your right, and that man you see over there is your husband." She complied and was immediately drawn to the handsome American. My mother's church was planted by the Conservative Baptist Association of America, so she was accustomed to seeing Americans. She never dreamed she would marry one, though. At the end of the service, my brave mother made her way to the front and introduced herself to the young man, knowing in her heart that this man would change her life forever. It was the beginning of a beautiful friendship that blossomed into an amazing love story.

My mother's commitment to her marriage was built on that Sunday morning experience. Their marriage—thirty-five years and counting—has been tested, tried, and proved. They have weathered storms, sickness, poverty, friction, and conflict, yet remain committed to the vow they made, that sacred covenant with God.

Their courtship could rival many Hollywood love stories. Conflicting obligations placed James in the jungle and Celia in the city. Undaunted, they wrote each other love letters for over a year. From jungle to city and city to jungle, each message was another thread woven into the tapestry of their blossoming love story, simultaneously expressing and strengthening it. When they were finally able to marry, friends and family pitched in to pay for Dad's suit, the food, and the cake. The humble reception took place right across the street at my mom's house. Simple ceremony, simple reception, but complex was the bond that united them. In addition to love and faith, they also shared a dream for the future: serving Christ as missionaries.

Soon after their honeymoon, my parents began their life together in the primitive wilds of the Amazon. Homesteading and living strictly off the land, they started to build what

I now remember as paradise in the middle of the Amazon Rainforest. The work was hard, and the young couple faced major difficulties. For starters, my mother was a city girl! She was raised in Manaus, the Amazon's capital city. She had never liked the outdoors, but she loved God and she loved my dad, so she followed both into the jungle. She believed in my father's dream and willingly joined in the unfamiliar adventure. Mother eventually accepted the less-than-ideal living conditions but never thoroughly enjoyed them. For example, it was not unusual to look up from her bed at the mosquito netting and see large tarantulas hanging over her. To this day, she hates tarantulas. Even though they aren't poisonous, their prickly black hair can burn one's skin with itching and fiery pain similar to poison ivy. She also told tales of snakes that she encountered *inside* the home, hissing as they stared at her from their hiding places. I can only imagine my mom's terror, but I have a feeling that it was eclipsed by her tenacity—and her confidence that she was in God's will.

Unlike my mom, my dad has always loved the primitive lifestyle. My parents' first home was made of red clay, with palm leaves for a roof. All their food was produced and cultivated in their back yard.

Envision with me, for a moment, those choices my parents made early in their marriage. When they chose the land where they would build their home, they didn't pick a neighborhood the way Americans do. They didn't stroll through a developed area with cookie-cutter houses, neat sidewalks, and decorative fences. Their "neighborhood" was a shifting scramble of dirt roads and farmland scraped into the jungle. If there was any concrete, it was probably part of a bridge. They were surrounded by the dense Amazon Rainforest, where monkeys and crickets competed with frogs in a truly surreal screaming contest. For a little family settling down at night in pitch-black darkness, those eerie sounds were a reminder that something unknown could be crawling toward you at any time. This jungle was my parents' reality and home. Soon it would be mine and my brothers' as well.

I know my grandparents and my parents did great things, and my parents are still missionaries (currently in Africa), yet they all experienced failures and setbacks. They did not surrender, but pressed on believing that God could use them to make a difference in the lives of others. Wherever my parents served, they shared Christ, made disciples, and planted churches. They also taught the locals how to make bricks, dig wells, and farm. They knew that God looked past perceived limitations—such as lack of money or education—and straight to their willing hearts. 1 Samuel 16:7b NIV reads, "The Lord does not look at the things people look at. People look at the outward appearance, but the Lord looks at the heart." We may face failures and setbacks on the road to seeing our dreams fulfilled, but we cannot give up. These stories are my heritage, my dreams through generations. Their lives have built the foundation of who I am, what I believe, and what my dreams are.

Take a moment to stop and think about where you came from. Who were your parents? Your grandparents? What did they become? What type of jobs did they have? How have these stories impacted you?

Take heart. No matter your answers, dreams can come true for you. Perhaps there are some aspects of your family legacy that you are not fond of. Every family has its own dysfunction. We all have faced conflict or shame in our families. Maybe divorce or estrangement or abuse has impacted you and your family. Though hurt and pain may be part of your story, God can still weave a beautiful tapestry that can inspire others and glorify Him. You can live a great adventure and be the best version of you. Whatever your story is, it is what makes you unique and your dreams personal to you. Embrace your past and let it be a launching pad to your destiny.

247 Acres

You who are young, be happy while you are
young, and let your heart give you joy in the
days of your youth.

—Ecclesiastes 11:9a NIV

My four brothers and I loved to go on adventures,
exploring the 247 acres surrounding our home:
Avilá. We scampered, laughed, and chased each
other in the blazing Amazon sunshine on a regular basis.
In our childlike thinking, this paradise was our own private
playground—but we were not alone. One day, I sensed another
adventure when I noticed something shiny under a dead tree.
Was it a mirror? (It reflected the sun perfectly.) Maybe it was
gold! Wow—lost Amazon treasure hundreds of years old—
could it be? All five of us ran closer to investigate. As fast as
our feet raced to our newfound treasure, our imaginations
raced faster.

But something wasn't right.

Did our sparkling treasure just move?

Nah.

Or did it?

You know that feeling you get when your eyes catch something but your brain doesn't understand it yet? That nagging sense that something isn't right? We associate it with realizing that you just drove past where you were supposed to turn; or remembering—*after* you walk in the classroom—that you have a test and you haven't studied; or, in my case, realizing that your exuberant brothers were flitting straight toward the fatal embrace of a fifteen-foot boa constrictor.

Yep, that was the feeling I had! Strangely enough, as my brothers neared their treasure, they began to have the same feeling. Our childlike glee vanished into fear.

Whenever we are stressed, we revert to our habits and stick with what is familiar. Well, our habit was to run to our father whenever we had a problem. And we had a fifteen-foot problem. We didn't have to think. We didn't have to agree on a plan of action. We *ran*.

"*Daddy!*"

Dad was our superhero and protector of the home. When he heard our story, he grabbed his gun and led us back to reclaim our paradise. Unafraid, he stayed between us and our adversary. The familiar *boom* of my father's rifle let us know that Daddy had rescued us again. To confirm the size of the prize, my father took a picture of us holding the dead snake. I clutched the head of the now powerless serpent while my brothers held up the rest of the dead body. Blood dripped between my toes, and I gleefully smiled for the camera. Fear was vanquished. My hero had slain the monster! (Just another day in the life of a jungle girl.)

I ran to my daddy when I had a problem because it was a habit. Develop the habit of running to your heavenly Father when you have a problem. Every problem. Every time. Proverbs 18:10 NLT promises, "The name of the LORD is a strong fortress; the godly run to Him and are safe." We are not, however, promised safety when we run *away* from God.

Is your problem too big for you? That's okay, because no problem is too big for God. Just as Daddy fought our battle for us that day, your heavenly Father fights for you. Be encouraged by Deuteronomy 20:4 NIV: "For the LORD your God is the one who goes with you to fight for you against your enemies to give you victory." You're not alone, because He goes with you, and you're not a loser, because He gives you victory. And remember, God knows a thing or two about defeating serpents that steal paradise. First Corinthians 15:57 NIV reads, "But thanks be to God! He gives us the victory through our Lord Jesus Christ."

One more thought before I move on: we don't find joy in the absence of problems. We find joy in the presence of God. Once I reached my daddy—although the snake (my problem) was still alive—my fear gave way to hope because I was in my father's presence. Listen to Psalm 16:11 NIV: "You make known to me the path of life; you will fill me with joy in your presence, with eternal pleasures at your right hand." Your joy is as close as the presence of your heavenly Father. Run to Him and be safe. *Daddy!*

As I mentioned earlier, my childhood paradise was a 247-acre farm called Avilá. Two hundred and forty-seven acres of jungle surrounded me as a little girl. Two hundred and forty-seven acres of adventure, love, hope, and dreams formed me into who I am today. On this land, my parents raised five children and sacrificed for us daily. They taught us faith and truth, love and courage, hard work and patience. My childhood—full of crazy jungle adventures and sobering life lessons—forged me into the dreaming Amazon girl I am today.

My parents' family grew rapidly. After three months of married life, my mom and dad found out they were expecting their first child: Bryan. When Bryan was three months old, mom became pregnant with twins: Edwin and me. You would think the biggest threat to my life as a child would be that boa constrictor. Nope, it was a lowly mosquito—and I wasn't even born yet. Mosquitoes are vile little creatures that transmit diseases such as yellow fever and malaria, killing more than two million people worldwide each year. Most of these outbreaks are confined to tropical areas, but guess what? It doesn't get much more tropical than the Amazon Rainforest. Because of a mosquito bite, Mom contracted malaria while carrying us. With no prenatal care, she became gravely ill. She wasted away to just skin and bones. Mom has always said it's a miracle that my brother and I survived the pregnancy. Don't forget, she was also taking care of a baby boy. The only time she was able to check on our development was when she visited her parents in Manaus. A midwife touched her belly and told her exactly how we were doing. No blood work. No sonograms. Just—poke—a touch on the belly. Late in her pregnancy, during one such visit, Dad wanted to return to the jungle, but the midwife insisted that Mom stay because the birth was so close. That midwife was right! My brother and I were born February 26,

inside the fruit like wedges in an orange. God is such an amazing artist, isn't He? Just one tree produces about 250 pounds of nuts every year. Since they live well beyond 500 years, I think of how the world around my Brazil nut tree has changed again and again in its lifetime. But every year it gets a little bigger, a little stronger, and a little more fruitful. Now I realize that majestic tree in my yard was a constant reminder of spiritual growth, longevity, and fruitfulness. Reminders we put on our refrigerator or smartphones can be overlooked. God's reminders—such as a massive Brazil nut tree in your back yard—are pretty hard to miss. If we plant our roots deep in our local church, we can mature into a stable, fruitful influence that's impossible to ignore.

Although the rainforest surrounding our farm was something of a wonderland, it could also be a dense, damp, and scary environment. Eerie noises wafted through the trees. They sounded like humans in despair, but I never investigated to see what they really were. I grew up hearing Amazon myths and legends that have frightened small children for generations. These stories crippled me with fear, and I never entered the deep, uncharted jungle alone. Just because our world was beautiful didn't mean it was safe. My brothers and I ran to our father a lot!

What's a jungle farm without animals? When people in the United States want a pet, they might go to a shelter, a big box pet store for Adoption Saturday, or even a breeder. My brothers and I simply went into the jungle, made friends, and brought them home. For example, I had two beautiful red macaws and a monkey named Oscar—all from the jungle. Maybe one reason

we kept going to the jungle for new pets was that our non-jungle pets kept dying. I had a cat that wandered into the jungle one day and never returned. And then there was my fluffy, adorable baby chick I loved to snuggle. I always kept it close to me. I even let it sleep with me. I learned—painfully—one advantage of sleeping with teddy bears instead of live chickens: when you roll on top of teddy bears in your sleep, they don't suffocate and die. I was devastated. These animals definitely taught me responsibility—at times the hard way. (Poor little chick!)

As we lived on a working farm, we also had a horse, cattle, and—ahem—chickens. There is nothing like drinking a cold cup of fresh milk once it has cooled down after boiling. Our corral was actually a two-story building. The cows stayed on the ground level, so the second level was yet another play area for me. There was a large wooden ramp leading to the top floor. Running up and down that ramp was one of my favorite pastimes. My brothers cleaned out the corral each morning after sending the cattle out to graze. Each afternoon before the sun set, Dad and our family dog would head out to the fields to bring the cows back, keeping them safe from the dangers of the Amazon. The farm required hard work, but for little kids, it felt like a theme park. My four brothers and I had the ultimate fun childhood. There was plenty of land to run on and explore, and—as I mentioned earlier—there were lots of animal friends to bring home. As the sister of four boys, I learned how to survive in the jungle, but I was still a princess in my parents' eyes—and, in my heart, a city girl.

By our tenth year on Avila, our humble farm had become a beautiful paradise, and we enjoyed the fruits of my parents'

labor—literally. Trees our parents had planted years ago now yielded fruit in great abundance: mangoes, grapefruit, lemons, tangerines, papayas, açai, pineapple, Brazil nuts, guavas, and inga. Inga was my favorite; they are so much fun to climb! Açai are full of natural antioxidants. Why didn't I think of importing some to the United States? We even enjoyed fresh honey from wild honeycombs. I was a great tree climber (maybe all that running up and down the corral ramp paid off), so it was my job to gather honey and fruit for our family.

Almost every day at lunchtime, my dad took us to a nearby stream. We ran and jumped and swung from vines right into the cold, dark water—clothes and all. No floats. No goggles. No lifeguards. This stream had fast currents, and swimming there turned us into strong swimmers. Dad kept a close eye on us, but we had to depend on our own abilities to stay above the water. Of course, he first taught us how to swim by simply tossing us in! Even at play, Dad taught us the skills necessary to survive deep in the Amazon Rainforest. Some daughters are taught to change tires on a car; I was taught to survive in the jungle.

Believe it or not, we also had a swimming pool—a *homemade* swimming pool. My dad formed broken pieces of asphalt into a floor and four walls, cemented and sealed everything, and—*voila!*—a pool large enough to hold ten children. Dad built the pool right next to our water well and installed a small hose so we could easily keep the pool filled. The inside lining was cement and painted with a bright blue oil-based paint. Today I marvel at my father's ingenuity and desire to give his children a wonderful life. He wanted us to have the best, even with simple resources.

My dad built the house I grew up in, but we were now in our second home. It was a beautiful two-story brick house with huge pillars surrounding the outside. The pillars were made from some of the strongest lumber the jungle had to offer: *muirapiranga*. We had a generator, but we only used it to give us light at night and cool the refrigerator. Our house had several bedrooms to comfortably accommodate all five children. My brothers shared their rooms, of course, but as the only girl, I had the perk of a bedroom all to myself.

Being the only girl had its drawbacks too. While my dad trained me to thrive in the wild, my mother made sure I was an expert at more domestic matters. Every day was laundry day. Each afternoon, I hung clothes and folded laundry. We didn't have the luxury of a dryer or other modern appliances, so I hung our clothes outside on a clothesline, relying on good sunny days to dry our clothes. I remember walking toward the clothesline, overwhelmed by the loads of laundry piled on my head and shoulders—there was no hamper or laundry basket. Being small, I would stretch and stand on my toes just to be able to reach the line, and then pile up the clothes on my shoulders and over my head to the point where I couldn't even see where I was going. I wanted to get this chore done all in one trip. The sun was scorching in the Amazon and burned my little head without pity. When the clothes were dry and I needed to go back to the house, I zigzagged like a bumblebee until I stumbled inside, nearly out of breath. I would throw the massive pile of laundry onto the bed and start folding, one piece at a time—which felt like it took an eternity. At least I was out of the sun! This hard work day after day, even at a young age, impressed upon me the importance of dedication and work ethic that I have relied upon throughout my years in ministry.

Our two-story house wasn't a fancy home, but it was a happy home. My dad made almost every piece of furniture we had! I learned that a building and possessions don't make a home. What makes a real home are parents who are involved in the lives of their children, loving and nurturing and raising them with a Christ-focused passion. My childhood was a great one, with lots of love and happy memories—but not absent of painful moments, which I'll share in the next chapter. Think back to your childhood. Which memories are most vivid to you: happy memories, or memories of abandonment and hurt? Whether happy or painful, your memories and experiences play a role in your development and journey.

You may be a young reader who is going through a tough, painful time. Can I just encourage you to remember that Jesus is right there with you? It's easy to believe that God is good and close when things are going great, but don't let the enemy fool you into thinking that God is far off when you are in a painful season.

> The Lord is near the brokenhearted; He saves those crushed in spirit.
> —Psalm 34:18 HCSB

His presence can provide peace even in the hardest times. Run to Him. I sure do, even now. *Daddy!*

When Hurt
Interrupts

Intense emotions create intense memories. Most Americans of a certain age remember where they were and how they felt on September 11, 2001. Very few, I dare say, remember September *10* as vividly. Some days—some *moments*—make a deeper impression on our hearts than others, as if they grip memory's pen a little tighter, press down on our souls a little harder, to ensure that we never forget.

I remember a particular Sunday afternoon when I was five. We were at the house of family who was very close to us in Manaus. My brothers and I played with the other kids. The grown-ups were out of sight and out of mind. After we played underneath the porch, we went inside for a nap. How carefree I felt as I slid across the waxed red floors of the living room! We all nestled into one big bed. In his deep voice, the male adult in the room pleaded with us to go to sleep.

I was almost asleep when I felt a firm grip on my ankles. He pulled me across the bed to him. My heart pounded in my ears. I couldn't move. I knew this wasn't right. I pretended to be asleep, but that didn't protect me. I finally realized, *I need to do something to get out of this.* I pretended to wake from sleep, and that's when he stopped. I turned over and curled up in the fetal position.

I remember I felt helpless and alone. I remember time stopped, each second lasting an eternity. I remember feeling unbearable emptiness after my innocence was cruelly ripped from me.

I remember it all.

He sexually abused me when I was five years old. That moment interrupted my sweet and carefree life. I would never be the same. I returned home, told no one, and tried to live the same way as before. I was deeply wounded, but I pushed the hurt far beneath the surface.

I tried to keep my distance from him, but seeing him was inevitable. He was, after all, someone we did life with. At least he lived in Manaus at that time, far away from Avila, far from my refuge—my sanctuary. There's just something about feeling safe and secure in your own home. Yet, in my own room, in my little wooden bed my father custom-built with his own hands for his little princess—where I felt safest—he struck again.

Early one morning, nearly five years after he first molested me, he crept into my room. We're supposed to wake up to escape nightmares, but that morning I woke up trapped inside a real, wide-awake one. I was paralyzed with fear, able to move only my eyes. All the pain and shame and torment I had pushed down—and all the feelings a little girl can't even articulate—came flooding back, overwhelming me. My blanket wasn't enough to cover my body, to protect me from this predator. I wanted to scream, to demand that he leave. Instead, my mouth dried up. His commanding presence controlled and intimidated me. As I lay there, all sense of security and hope drained out of me. I was trapped. I was helpless. I was prey. He got on my little-girl bed, leaned over me, and sexually abused me. With a cynical smirk on his face, he said words that I will never forget: "You have grown up quite a bit, turning into a young lady." How *dare* he say such a thing! Again, I wanted to scream for help, but I couldn't. Finally, he left. I can still see him turning his back and sneaking out so he wouldn't get caught. I turned over and wept bitterly. The torment was back. I had tried to suppress the hurts for so many years, but here they all were again, raw and inescapable. I began to hope that one day, as years went by, these painful memories would disappear forever.

Yet, as before, I remember it all.

Wounds heal, but scars remain.

No one goes through life without some kind of hurt. Some wounds are so deep that only God's healing balm can bring complete restoration. We wonder why God allows these hurts. I don't understand why, and I don't have a tidy answer that will magically make everything better. I do know, however, that God takes every bad experience, and He amazingly turns it around and uses it for the best—usually to help others.

As time went by, I found comfort in God alone. He reassured me many times that all things work for the good and His plan. When I was twenty years old—fifteen years after the first abuse—I could not keep this dark secret any longer. The only way to receive total freedom—and stop being a slave to my secret—was to share it with someone. I remember breaking the news to my best friend on my twentieth birthday. *At last!* The weight of the world fell off my shoulders. I was healing. I then told my parents, who were extremely upset and hurt by the news. I asked my parents to forgive him and move on, as I had already done. They did not dwell long on their own hurt. They saw the peace and freedom that God had given me about the entire traumatic experience.

Let me encourage you to examine your past with open eyes and an open heart. Unless you acknowledge and address those painful memories—and allow God to heal your wounds—those hurts will always be in your *now* rather than your *past*. You won't be able to move into the future in freedom. I meet lots of girls whose secret hurts hold them captive to the past. Their wounds are still open—covered up, but not healed. If only they could share with someone they trust—and ask for prayer—it would make all the difference. Believe me, I know how difficult it is, but I can promise you that the freedom on the other side is worth it. Allow our loving God to transform your hurt from your *story* to your *history*.

Scars are victory. Scars mean that the hurt is trapped in the past—and we aren't. We don't brush our past experiences under the rug or pretend that they don't affect us. It all matters, and it all counts. Some scars are so conspicuous that we could never hide them, but you get to choose how your story is told. The victim finds identity in past hurts. The victorious lets God redeem and repurpose those hurts to help others. The victim and the victorious look at the same scar; one sees hurt, while the other sees healing. Remember my list of dreams from chapter one? *Vitória*—victory—is on that list. God-given victories are won in the arena of the heart and the mind by faith—not by willpower or denial. God, through His mercy, has given me *vitória* over the hurt. If He did it for me, He can do it for you.

> For every child of God defeats this evil world,
> and we achieve this victory through our faith.
> —1 John 5:4 NLT

That's not the end of this story. On September 30, 2001, after I was already in bed, the phone rang. I heard a familiar deep voice. It was him. I was shocked and—hearing that voice again while I was in bed—I couldn't move. I tried to compose myself and hold a normal conversation with him. He called to apologize for the hurt and the pain that he had caused me. The call itself was an act of God. While he did not directly say "I am sorry," I knew that was the purpose of the phone call. I told him I forgave him, and that was the last time we ever spoke. That phone call gave me closure. I learned how to quit blaming myself for what happened. I learned to forgive myself for what had taken place, and I forgave him for violating me. I accepted the fact that those hurts in my childhood changed my life forever—but they don't define it. My history is not my identity.

When hurt interrupts our lives, we need to intentionally focus on the positive so we don't become bitter. Many times, we wonder why bad things happen to us. I stopped asking why many years ago. I know God takes every bad experience and somehow uses it for the best. Can all things really work themselves out for the best? If God says they can, then they can—and God doesn't lie. Romans 8:28 NIV assures, "And we know that in all things God works for the good of those who love him, who have been called according to his purpose." If you love Him and you are called, then all things will work out for your good.

I learned from my hurt that being molested built up a defense that helped keep me pure until the day I was married. I also learned that my past hurt inducted me into a sisterhood that is also my mission field. Because of the compassion that overflowed from my own healing, I have ministered to many young ladies who have been raped or molested. It has been beautiful to stand with them as they step out of their place of hurt and into a place of freedom and healing. I thank God for these positive consequences to my hurt that, at ages five and ten, I could not have foreseen. I learned that I am living out 2 Corinthians 1:4 NLT: "He comforts us in all our troubles so that we can comfort others. When they are troubled, we will be able to give them the same comfort God has given us." Now I actually thank God for having gone through these painful experiences because of all the good He has done. No matter how much I try, I cannot go back and change the past. I have accepted the fact that those hurts from my childhood changed my life, yet have made me stronger and even more compassionate for those who are hurting. I wasn't happy about the wounds, but I am thankful for the scars. Wounds heal, but scars remain. Scars are victory. *Vitória!*

What is your story? What is your pain? Here is a promise from Psalm 34:18 *Message:* "If your heart is broken, you'll find God right there; if you're kicked in the gut, he'll help you catch your breath." Does this verse describe you? Has your heart been broken? Did the pain make you feel as though you were kicked in the gut? I love how God can help us catch our breaths over and over again. He can help us move forward instead of remaining trapped in the past. When hurt disrupts our lives, it's easy to think we're all alone. But the Bible promises that God is right there, helping us catch our breaths. If we let the hurt isolate and control us, then it becomes our identity—a *false* identity. Our true identity is in Christ, and we need to showcase the splendor of His glory and not let hurt eclipse His light.

> For you are all children of God through faith in Christ Jesus.
>
> —Galatians 3:26 NLT

> You, LORD, keep my lamp burning; my God turns my darkness into light.
>
> —Psalm 18:28 NIV

> I have come as a light to shine in this dark world, so that all who put their trust in me will no longer remain in the dark.
>
> —John 12:46 NLT

You have turned my mourning into joyful dancing. You have taken away my clothes of mourning and clothed me with joy, that I might sing praises to you and not be silent. O Lord my God, I will give you thanks forever!

—Psalm 30:11–12 NLT

I have told you these things so that in me you may have peace. In this world you will have trouble. But take heart! I have overcome the world.

—John 16:33 NIV

Don't let hurt stop you from dreaming and living your life to its fullest. We can overcome any hurt with our God. He has overcome the world. God does not waste your experiences—including your hurts. Your story matters: from before you were born, to every childhood experience, to your life right now. Each aspect of my jungle childhood—including my hurt—has mattered. God used it all to shape me and my dreams. Despite my grown-up life now with a husband and three children, I still find that little jungle girl inside at times. She is still there, craving adventure. There's still a child in you. The child in you may need healing in order to dream again. If so, my prayer is that you take your hurt to Jesus and let Him do what only He can do.

Then Jesus said, "Come to me, all of you who
are weary and carry heavy burdens, and I will
give you rest."

—Matthew 11:28 NLT

Wounds heal, but scars remain. Scars are victory.
Vitória!

Rescue Mission

> I waited patiently for the LORD; he turned
> to me and heard my cry. He lifted me out of
> the slimy pit, out of the mud and mire; he set
> my feet on a rock and gave me a firm place
> to stand. He put a new song in my mouth,
> a hymn of praise to our God. Many will see
> and fear the LORD and put their trust in him.
>
> —Psalm 40:1–3 NIV

I marvel at all that my father's hands have made: our first home; nearly all of our furniture (including my bed); our church (with help, of course). Each design was for our good. Each structure was a sanctuary, a place of refuge.

I never questioned my father's ability as a carpenter. I never worried about the structural integrity of anything he built. As a child, my thought process was, "Daddy made it, so it's good." I never worried about our house collapsing on top of us as we ate breakfast or my bed shattering to splinters as I climbed into it. *Daddy made it, so it's good.*

When I reminisce about the church my father helped build, which was next door to our home, the first image in my mind's eye is of large floor-to-ceiling shutter windows. The Amazon is hot and humid, and there was no air conditioning, but those enormous shutter windows let fresh breezes circulate through the church. The second image is of my wonderful mother.

When I entered our church as a young girl, wearing my favorite dress, which my mother had sewn with her own hands, I would see my mother and notice how beautiful she was. She exuded passion and love. I didn't see her there as Mommy, but rather as a leader of our church. Her beautiful voice made sweet music with a tambourine. I knew that whatever she had, I wanted it! She was so happy and full of joy—I wanted to be just like her. When she asked me to sing with her, that was the beginning of my involvement in church. I looked forward to every Sunday evening. I would put on my favorite dress and run to church to sing with my mom. After worship, my dad would preach.

I grew up in church. I first heard about Jesus Christ in church. I gave my life to Him in church. As I grew up, I saw the local church as a beacon of hope to the poor and the hurting. The church was also a place where I grew and flourished—as did the congregants. I can still recall faces of individuals who helped my father build a large room out of bricks and cement, transforming it into a sanctuary in mere weeks. The design was efficient: a rectangular space with several large windows along the walls to keep the inside cool, a small stage for musicians facing the congregation, and always a nice wooden pulpit, usually built by my dad. Rustic and beautiful like the rainforest surrounding it, the church was an ideal setting for worship. I can close my eyes right now and see it in my memories.

What I remember most, and what I can still hear, are the laughter and happy noises of people excited to come to church. Most of the locals walked to church on red dirt roads—even when it rained. Our little church would still be packed on those days with hundreds of people—all with muddy feet. After services, our church floors would be covered in dried red mud. I'm reminded of Proverbs 14:4 NLT: "Without oxen a stable stays clean, but you need a strong ox for a large harvest." I grew up knowing that a church that is always clean is always empty. We were thankful for muddy floors. For those that lived too far to walk, my dad would drive our minibus and pack it to standing room only; there were no seat belts or car seats. As we rode along, the air was filled with an unforgettable blend of sweat, diesel fumes, and singing.

My parents' joy was contagious. I began to notice that our family was full of smiles and laughter. My five-year-old mind discerned: *we are a happy family.* As I got a little older and began to grasp what my dad was preaching, I understood why my parents were so passionate. I knew there was something drawing me to *more.* This *more to life* was my parents' reason for spurning the comforts and safety of living in America, the reason they poured their lives into a people who had nothing to offer them, the reason they built a church in a beautiful yet dangerous place. This *more to life* was the reason for everything they did.

Our little community was no match for the size of their faith and love, and I was drawn in along with everyone else.

Soon my enthusiasm shifted to curiosity. I paid attention and wanted to learn. At our little church I learned about Jesus, about eternity. I knew that I needed Him, but how could I know that I had Him in my heart? I wanted what my mom and dad had—and what they were giving to the natives. So when Dad preached about Jesus and asked if anyone wanted to ask Him into his or her heart, I went forward. I bowed my head and waited to see if something would happen. I felt happy, but I wasn't sure if I would go to heaven. After that service, I could barely wait until next Sunday. Again, Dad preached about Jesus. Again, I made my way up the aisle. Again, I bowed my head and closed my eyes. But this time, I prayed to Jesus and asked Him to please come into my heart and take me to heaven when I die. This time, I knew something happened. I felt an assurance and a confidence that I had never felt before. Jesus met me that day and filled my heart. I knew at that moment that I was connected with eternity, and—if I died—I knew where I was going.

Even now this incredible experience has left me in awe. In my world, the Amazon Rainforest, there are *30 million* different species of insects. There are snakes the size of cars and trees as tall as skyscrapers. It's easy in such an environment to feel small, insignificant, even *overlooked*. And to think that my beloved Avila was just a tiny part of Brazil, which is just one country on earth, which is just one planet in our solar system, which is just a speck of dust compared to the entire universe—well, it can be overwhelming.

Until you know the Creator.

God, the Creator of all things, took the time to go on a rescue mission deep in the Amazon Rainforest for a poor, weak, skin-and-bones, wild-haired, dirty-cheeked, barefooted child. For *me*. The same year someone nearly destroyed me, my Savior rescued me. It makes me want to cry tears of joy. I was headed to a life of loss and despair—honestly, going straight to hell. But because Jesus loves me, He lined up saved generations before me (my grandparents, my parents) to lead me into the big plan He dreamt up all along: a rescue mission to save me from eternal destruction. And He used a village to make it happen.

He did it for me, and He can do it for you. You are not overlooked. You matter. You have eternal worth and value. Your world may seem big to you, but it's not too big for God. After all, He made it. He knows where you are. He knows your name. He loves you so much that He died for you. (No one else has to, including you.) Jesus, by allowing Himself to be crucified, paid the price with His life to free you from every hurt, every sin, every shame. And He rose from the dead to prove that everyone who believes in Him will live forever with Him in heaven. When you let Jesus rescue you, you have nothing to lose but your chains, plus freedom and heaven to gain. There is *more to life,* and His name is Jesus.

> For God loved the world so much that he gave his one and only Son, so that everyone who believes in him will not perish but have eternal life.
>
> —John 3:16 NLT

> If you confess with your mouth, "Jesus is
> Lord," and believe in your heart that God
> raised Him from the dead, you will be saved.
> —Romans 10:9 HCSB

Giving my life to Christ and surrendering my heart to Him gave me a whole new perspective on life. There was purpose behind going to church now. I started to understand "the why" behind what my parents did. They knew how important it was for us to grow up in a healthy church environment, so we could see for ourselves that a spiritually abundant life was something real and available; it wasn't some mysterious concept that was only for other people in other places. It was for *me*. And it's for *you*. I also had a new passion: everything within me wanted to introduce others to this amazing heavenly Father, the one I met in that little church tucked in the deep, dense forest. I was astounded and grateful that the Creator of heaven and earth cared about me. I was only a child, but I mattered to Him. So do you.

As was his custom, Dad loaded up new converts in his gray bus to be baptized in the river. Bicycles and canoes were the main forms of transportation, so riding in a bus was a luxury. Our bus was one of a kind. Dad, a man of many talents, is also an artist. He loves to draw, and on the back of our bus he painted a picture of a lion and wrote in large bold words, *Leão da Tribo de Judá:* "Lion of the tribe of Judah." Jesus is called this in the Bible in Revelation 5:5.

Baptism was a huge event. After arriving at the site, we gathered at a wooden bridge. There was no concrete here, and the sides of the bridge were painted white so that it would be more visible to river traffic. We had no worries about street traffic. We were in the jungle, and few cars traveled this highway (BR-319). I walked down from the bridge along the edges of the muddy hill and made my way into the peaceful river. Surrounded by the family and friends I loved, I was baptized. So many of us were baptized that day that the water was muddied by the time we finished. Children played along the water's edge in canoes; adults sang; everyone celebrated.

Being baptized was a turning point in my life; I was making a public announcement that I was a new creation in Jesus. I buried "the old me" (without Jesus in my heart) in the river, and I resolved that "the new me" would never turn my back on my rescuer. It amazes me that as a child I did not doubt, and when faced with the grand power of God, I just believed. Talking to Him became a regular habit for me. I knew He listened and heard every word I said. When I gave my heart to Jesus, my eyes were opened to a whole new world. I was now a part of a kingdom without borders or limitations, where the impossible is made possible.

God is on a rescue mission for you. He will use others and circumstances to guide you to a moment of decision. We all have the same choice: we either agree to be rescued or remain in our chains. My prayer is that you will place your faith in Jesus Christ: the one and only who can fill you with perfect, unconditional love; the one and only who can give you a purpose and a dream greater than you imagine. He left the flawless splendor of heaven because He loved a fallen, damaged world. He humbled Himself to become a mere human so He could feel what we feel. He understands. He *gets it.* When you think no one understands, no one cares, no one knows… Jesus *does.* Christ became one of us so each of us could become one of His.

Remember how I said I never questioned my father's ability as a carpenter? How I trusted that neither my bed nor my house would fall apart? I didn't know anything about woodworking or carpentry, but I knew my daddy. *Daddy made it, so it's good.* Well, God has big dreams and plans for you—for your life both on earth and in heaven. You may not understand every single detail, but when God does it, it's good!

"For I know the plans I have for you," declares the LORD, "plans to prosper you and not to harm you, plans to give you hope and a future."

—Jeremiah 29:11 NIV

"Your heart must not be troubled. Believe in God; believe also in Me. In My Father's house are many dwelling places; if not, I would have told you. I am going away to prepare a place for you. If I go away and prepare a place for you, I will come back and receive you to Myself, so that where I am you may be also."

—John 14:1–3 HCSB

First church my parents built on our farm
Avilá, next door to our house.

Church baptism under wooden bridge in
the heart of the Amazon Jungle.

Parents and my four brothers on our farm
Avilá. Brazil nut tree in the background.

Public transportation down the Amazon River.

My dad, James Williams, with his family on
the mission field. Dad, top right corner.

My brothers and me with a boa constrictor
my dad killed on our farm.

Uncharted Roads

I f we wanted to travel anywhere in the Amazon, we had two options: poorly maintained roads or the Amazon River. Whenever we drove to the city, our van would bump and rock along the treacherous highway, hitting potholes the size of kiddie pools every few minutes. Each time we hit a hole, we kids bounced around, bumping into each other and laughing. One evening, my dad spotted a pothole that was too big to miss, yet too big to hit. As we sloshed to a halt, we noticed that this was no pothole; the road had completely washed out.

Remember, my dad was a farmer as well as a missionary, so he was an expert problem solver. Farmers—especially missionary farmers in the middle of the Amazon—learn to be part veterinarian, part plumber, part electrician, part mechanic, part whatever-is-needed. When problems arise, farmers learn to solve them or else. Let's say you're in the middle of nowhere, it's getting dark, and the road is out; what do you do? Turn around and go home? Not when you can build a bridge.

Using the van, dad started dragging logs into place. Unfortunately, before he could finish, the universal drive on the van broke. This thwarted our bridge building project and crippled our van. We were stranded. While our parents waited for help to come along, we kids dove into muddy potholes and splashed around, getting filthy. Of course, we had to get clean, so we'd find the closest body of water and wash off. What a blast!

Time passed, but help didn't come. As daylight faded, we dined on what we had: Spam. As we finished our meal, darkness fell with a thud. Had a giant blanket just been thrown over the treetops? There was no moon, no stars, just darkness.

We saw nothing and heard everything. Some sounds we recognized: wild hogs, a jaguar (my biggest fear), and the usual chants and screams that make up the primal jungle orchestra. Other sounds were unfamiliar, eerie. We weren't having a blast anymore. We felt disconnected, vulnerable, *afraid*. What if something came out of the forest? If we couldn't see, how could we know whether one of us wandered off?

We did have a visitor that night, and thankfully, it wasn't a jaguar. An older man approached us by the roadside. He seemed very sweet and friendly and had a gentle smile. Although he was a stranger, he invited us to his home. We could not resist the offer, so—weary and dirty—we followed him home. I remember walking up a long dirt driveway that led to a small wooden house with a silvery tin roof. As our large family crowded into this tiny house, I remember the pleasant smell of an antique wood-burning stove. The kind stranger took us in, served us a warm dinner, and insisted we spend the night. We were safe and secure. What a blessing that sweet old man was to us! That episode challenged me to notice others in need, to never get numbed to others' pain. We need to practice hospitality in every environment by making others feel warm, welcome, and included.

Sometimes the roads on our life journey are riddled with holes, obstacles, and waiting periods. It's easy to question why our hopes and dreams are taking so long, but I encourage you to look around, enjoy the pause, and keep moving toward your goal. Who knows? A Good Samaritan might surprise you with help and comfort when you need it most.

At other times, roads on our life journey close, and we have to choose a new path. Sadly, this is what happened to my family. I'm being literal here: road conditions were so dangerous that the government *shut down* the main highway near our home. Closed it. Forever. No more highway. This was catastrophic to our humble community. Imagine if the government shut down 95 percent of the transportation connecting your city or town to the outside world. Goods to purchase, job opportunities, customers for local businesses—these revenue streams would simply flow elsewhere, to people and places easier to reach. That's what happened to us. Once the highway shut down, our local economy flowed away—and took most of the population with it. Transporting crops from the farmlands to the city became functionally impossible. Farmers like us could no longer make a living. Our roadside produce stand no longer had a road. Our community disintegrated in mere weeks. This was the end of Avila, the only home I knew. This was also the end of our church, our farm, our income, our neighbors, our whole world. Circumstances beyond our control uprooted us from everything except each other, and this was hard for me to handle. Reluctantly, we relocated to the nearest city, Humaitá. Heartbroken, we started over from nothing.

Leaving the grandeur of the rainforest for the grit of the city felt like moving from the garden of Eden to a plastic flowerpot. The confines of urban life clashed with our jungle lifestyle. At times, it felt like we traded 247 acres for 247 next-door neighbors, but we made the best of it. The lot we lived on was next to a wooded area, and that soon became our favorite playground. We made a bike trail where we would ride and play all day long.

Many equate being a missionary with primitive living in remote areas. To me, our rustic life on Avila was normal. It wasn't difficult; it was home. Ironically, it was in the city that I learned what it meant to be a missionary. My parents taught us that we were born to fulfill a purpose greater than ourselves. This mission required a willing heart and radical love for God. Looking back at our forced exodus from the rainforest, I know that God used this painful transition to send me to my very first mission field: public school in Humaitá. I had to learn the lesson of "doing things afraid." I had to learn to face fear and not cower to it. This lesson would stay with me throughout many new roads that I would travel later in life.

Mother homeschooled us when we lived on Avila, but those days were gone. Public school was an eye-opening experience. It was like Sodom and Gomorrah to sheltered jungle children like us. God had first place in my heart, but remaining faithful to Him was easy in the isolated safety of Avila. Now, at age twelve, for the first time in my young life, I was being called to shine and show my faith to a dark and intimidating world.

I was an outsider in just about every way. The students were terrible: sex, drugs, and foul language were the norm. And my professor? To this day, he stands out as one of the most profane, filthy-mouthed people I have ever met. Shocked but not surprised, I realized that we lived in a dark world filled with hurting people. Our parents had taught us about the reality of the world we lived in, one of fallen humanity that desperately needed Jesus. They were right: my whole school needed Jesus!

Nothing was easy. Even an adolescent crush turned ugly. A boy in my school liked me. He was older and street smart, and he thought a naive tomboy from the jungle would be an easy catch. When I refused him, he became hostile. His "love" turned to hate, his flirting changed to bullying, and his bullying grew into stalking. Everywhere I went, he was there, taunting me, threatening me. He was obsessed with me. He lived to harass and intimidate me. One day, as I was walking home from school, he sped down a hill and struck me with his bicycle, injuring my arm. After that, my mom decided it was too dangerous for me to travel to and from school on my own, so she had one of our friends on the police force take me to school—and threaten the bully to leave me alone. I don't know what the police officer said to him, but that bully never bothered me again.

My brothers and I are proof that if you teach your children the ways of Jesus and model what it's like to be a Christ-follower, your children will be strong enough not to compromise their morals when they are sent out into a dark world. Proverbs 22:6 NIV promises, "Start children off on the way they should go, and even when they are old they will not turn from it." So we learned the balance of adapting to the culture without compromising our values.

I knew I had to be a light. I had learned about letting "this little light of mine" shine. Jesus said in Matthew 5:14 that we are the light of the world. I think of the sun and how it warms and illuminates us and never stops shining. We use terms like *sunrise* and *sunset* as if the sun comes and goes, but it never truly leaves us. What really happens is that we turn away from the light and into darkness. And when we turn back, the light that was always there warmly welcomes us. Following this model, I let my light shine on those around me, even when they turned their backs on me. Was I bullied, mocked, ridiculed? Sure. Was there pressure to "hide my light"? Of course. But how can you hide the sun? Or the Son that spoke it into existence? My mission was greater than me, and so was the one who sent me. I could not deny or hide my relationship with Christ any more than I could prevent the sun from shining. So I relied on Jesus. As I said, "doing things afraid" was the lesson I had to learn. Courage is not the absence of fear. Courage is acting despite the fear. Sometimes you have to let go of what's comfortable and familiar and boldly follow Christ Jesus on paths that only He sees. Remember, when you follow Jesus, everywhere you are, He's already been. If He hadn't led me into such a dark place, I wouldn't have known how bright my little light could shine. My life in Humaitá taught me to embrace—not resist— change and new seasons. Ultimately, life is one season after another, with the next one always on the horizon.

Have you ever seen the horizon on the water? It seems to beckon you to new adventures. During our stay in Humaitá, I spent a lot of time gazing at the horizon on the river. The public boat system was the cheapest and safest way to travel, so we were on the river all the time. The boats were always overcrowded, with strangers jam-packed in hammocks and stacked up like sardines in a can. Walking up to the boats, we would see children bathing near the dock in the filthy, contaminated water, swimming among feces and garbage. The sight always made me sick. We tried to arrive early to grab a good spot for our hammocks, avoiding the lower deck near the portable toilets at all costs, knowing that after a few days the stench would become unbearable and the ammonia vapors would burn our eyes like fire. This was no luxury cruise!

Despite the foul odors and bad food, the boats provided great views of the natural beauty of the Amazon River. I would stand along the bow of the boat, alone in my thoughts, full of wonder at the size and scenery of this massive, never-ending waterway. I enjoyed watching the *botos* (pink dolphins) swim alongside the boat, especially in the late afternoons. (The sunset was my favorite time of day. One day, the sun appeared so huge that it seemed only a few yards away.) Tropical birds added vivid color and a vibrant soundtrack to our journey. One moment, I would see a toucan pecking on a tree; the next, I would spy, flying high over the forest, red and blue macaws—which reminded me of the ones I had growing up on the farm. As always, the shrill, rhythmic cries of the golden parakeets put a smile on my face.

While I was watching birds and dolphins, Mom and Dad watched over souls. My parents delighted in having a captive audience, taking the opportunity to share Jesus with their fellow passengers. What a great place for missionaries! Mom often befriended all the women and helped sick children get back to health. People often asked if she was a doctor—and maybe she almost was. After having five kids of her own, she had lots of training.

Looking back at those boat trips, I can see how much my parents loved people. In the midst of floating squalor, they focused on the beauty of people created in the image of God, enriching them with the love of Jesus. Wherever you are on your journey, look around. Don't overlook the souls and scenery God has placed in your path. The beauty you find on the way to your dreams just might be the fuel you need to keep going.

Sometimes life can be like those boat rides. Passengers had to put their full trust in the captain, believing without doubting that he would bring them to their destination. My family and I had to extend that same trust each time we stepped onto a boat. We need to put our trust in God in the same way, knowing that the Holy Spirit will lead us and never forsake us. It won't always be easy sailing. Trials and challenges *will* come at us. After all, God sends His light where it's needed most: into darkness, and darkness hates the light (John 3:19–20). Instead of resisting hardship, recognize that the hardship is evidence that you're exactly where God wants you.

After I turned thirteen, our parents encouraged us kids to leave Humaitá to attend boarding school near Manaus, over four hundred miles away. Located on the banks of the Amazon River, Puraquequara (which everyone called PQQ) educated the children of tribal missionaries of New Tribes Mission, and had all grades K–12. This boarding school was a chance to learn English, which our parents knew would be valuable in the future. My dad let me decide whether or not I would attend. Although he did not force me to leave home, he did strongly encourage me to take advantage of this opportunity.

After reading about my unpleasant experiences in public school, you might think leaving a tough urban environment for a Christian utopia on the Amazon would be an easy decision, but it wasn't. In Humaitá, I could retreat from the stresses of life and hide in my sanctuary: home sweet home. I wouldn't have that at PQQ. I realized this was a crossroads for me. After a few weeks of talking and praying, I chose to leave along with my two older brothers. Little did I know that PQQ would become my next uncharted road.

The evening we departed for Puraquequara, my brothers and I huddled with our parents on a pier like migratory birds sharing a roost, temporary, fleeting. We had always followed them, first as wobbly ducklings, later soaring in formation, ever united. When seasons changed, we flew away together— always. This time, however, the season would change only for my brothers and me; it was time to fly on our own. As the boat eased into the night, leaving my parents behind, I realized they and I, for the first time, were moving in opposite directions, out of sync, out of sight. Feeling intense pain at this separation, unable to stand, I could only sit on a wooden bench and wave. I stared intently at my parents until the tears and the twilight blurred them into wavy mists and I couldn't see them anymore. I wanted to swim back into their loving arms, but deep down I knew that this path, though unfamiliar, was the right one.

When we arrived at PQQ, I was fear-stricken, and all I wanted to do was stay close to my brothers. They were the only familiar faces. American missionary kids speaking English surrounded us. I could barely understand anything they were saying. They all seemed so happy; it was like a big family reunion—yippee! But I felt lost, disconnected, a foreigner in my own country.

Spreading over gentle hills rising from the riverbank, the campus itself was lovely: tidy brick houses, lush lawns landscaped with fruit trees, sidewalks lined with fragrant flowers. As we walked toward our dorms, we passed through a small village where the faculty and their families lived in cute houses, all built alike. When I reached my dorm, which was at the very back of the campus, my kind dorm parents greeted me with a warm smile and showed me where my new bedroom was: the first room on the right of a long corridor. Squeezed into the cramped space were a bunk bed, a tiny wooden dresser, a small closet, and my roommate (standing up). She was very sweet, and I can still picture her in my mind: tall and slim with beautiful blue eyes and silky golden hair cut in a bouncy bob. She thankfully knew Portuguese, and whenever she spoke English, she would talk very slowly to make sure that I understood. After brief introductions, I made my bed, straightened my side of the room, and then cried myself to sleep. Classes began the next day.

The first few weeks of class were brutal. I sat next to my twin brother, Edwin, in front near the window. Overwhelmed, I could only stare out the window at the American flag, desperately trying to hide my silent tears. Placed in fifth grade after testing, I was, at thirteen, two to three years older than my classmates. Feeling awkward, humiliated, and hopelessly out of place, that bubbly, outgoing girl I used to be on Avila was now a quiet, sad child. After school and on weekends, while my classmates ran and played and laughed and thrived, I sat in a rocking chair for hours, alone in my thoughts. Other times, hoping to talk to my family, I sat by the phone, waiting, waiting. Learning this strange language, succeeding in this strange place—they both felt impossible. I wanted to go home, where I felt comfortable and loved. Loneliness pervaded my spirit, and I thought I would never fit in.

In spite of my homesickness and despair, I knew—somewhere *far* beneath my emotions—that I wasn't alone; Jesus was still with me. Because of His presence, hope began to flicker. Listen to Jeremiah 15:7–8 NIV: "But blessed is the one who trusts in the LORD, whose confidence is in him. They will be like a tree planted by the water that sends out its roots by the stream. It does not fear when heat comes; its leaves are always green. It has no worries in a year of drought and never fails to bear fruit." God plants us, but we have to send out our roots; we have to dig in. God had His hand on me; when I was uprooted from the Eden of Avila, when I was crammed into the plastic flowerpot of Humaitá, and when He transplanted me to this mini-America on the Amazon known as PQQ.

God planted me by the water, but it was my job to send out my roots; so I dug in.

After a few weeks, I made my mind up to embrace my new life and learn English, and was assigned a tutor to help with this crazy new language. Once again, I had to "do things afraid." I still missed my parents and younger brothers dearly, but now I had courage to face this new season. Slowly, eventually, fruit began to appear: peace budded—even joy—that didn't seem possible those first few weeks.

I attended school all day, study hall all evening, and the library when I could. Within four weeks, I was beginning to understand English and converse with my new friends. My life was changing. I was beginning to grow into a young adult; I had no choice but to grow up fast and be responsible—much like I learned to swim by being tossed into a river. PQQ was a school of about a thousand students, and with time, it started to feel like home. I was surrounded by people who loved God, which added to the family atmosphere. They had joy and peace and a love for Jesus just like I did. Also, there was a church where we gathered every Sunday morning. Church was a little different from what I was accustomed to. I grew up singing from hymnals full of beautiful, slow songs; in this church, I learned that variety of worship is a beautiful thing. God's presence compels us to worship, and that worship can take many different forms. New seasons bring new roads, and new roads create new worship.

I grew to love the school and everything it stood for. Since we were all children of missionaries and knew how to serve in our local communities, we were comfortable enough to meet with the locals and invite them to our gatherings. Sharing the love of Jesus, we served the community near the school just as our parents served back home; it was church in its simplest form.

I spent my free time with other students hiking, canoeing, and swimming in the Amazon River. During the rainy season, footpaths in the nearby forest would flood, creating ideal waterways for canoeing. Gliding through the flooded rainforest was enchanting. As we floated through infinite shades of green, the orchids seemed to burst with electric hues of lavender and purple. The cool shade of the forest canopy provided relief from the constant humidity. This felt like our own private paradise. I would take in several deep breaths, filling my lungs with clean air bathed in the dreamy fragrance of countless tropical flowers. The most beautiful sight of all looked like a ball of brilliant blue light bouncing magically through the air: it was a butterfly as large as the birds. I was mesmerized by its otherworldly beauty.

As much as I loved being with people and craved that sense of belonging, another part of me needed solitude. I enjoyed exploring, looking for a secret hiding place where I could get alone with God to pray, ponder, and be still. A child of the jungle, I bypassed the hiking path near the school and sought out the highest vantage point. From my secret spot I would sit and enjoy the panorama, looking down at this small community of teachers and missionary kids that had become my home. I could see the entire campus: all the buildings plus the outdoor basketball court and soccer field. Stomach growling, mouth watering, I would look at the cafeteria and think of our fresh homemade coffee cake loaded with brown sugar and melted butter—yum! Beyond our school flowed the majestic Amazon River. From my special spot, the river looked calm, yet I knew it was powerful with strong currents and teemed with life—and death. Boats passed by, carrying people, produce, and animals to new destinations. They all looked so clean from a distance, but they were quite the opposite, as I knew!

Allow me to use this panorama to share some perspective. What you see at a distance is never the whole story, whether scenery or souls. Relationship—and ministry—happens up close. You can't wipe tears or hold the hurting or carry the broken from a distance; you must be up close, in their world, in their lives. Paths lead to people, to community. I was much happier at church and on outreaches than I was alone in that rocking chair. We all need time to reflect and recharge; even Jesus went off by Himself to pray, but God's paths for us always lead to people. We need them; they need us; and we all need Jesus.

Amazon Meets America

I can't tell you what my teacher said because I didn't understand the words, but I can tell you how they sounded, how they felt: they were terrifying. I didn't know why she was angry with me, but I knew that she was—the way a dog knows when it's being scolded. She dragged me to the school attic, jabbing her finger toward my knees, my skirt. *Why am I in trouble? Is it because my uniform was used, worn by another girl last year?* She grabbed a musty old skirt that would probably fit the Statue of Liberty. *So is mine too short?* I had to take off my skirt—right there, in front of her—and put on that other, dingy, dusty one. Out of her torrent of words, I fished out "better." This giant skirt—which covered my ankles and had to be pinned because it wrapped around my waist—was *better.* Later, at recess, rather than flap around the playground in my *better* skirt, I sat on a bench, ashamed, watching the other kids have fun. Why humiliate me? Why not send a note home to my mother, explaining my skirt was too short? After all, Mom was an expert seamstress; she could have fixed it. Feeling self-conscious, feeling poor, feeling "less than," I made the situation worse with poisonous thoughts: *poor missionary kid; can't speak English; can't afford a snack for my lunch box; can't afford a new uniform; I hate school.*

Welcome to first grade in America.

This was my first impression of school in the United States. Our family was there on furlough, which is a year-long home assignment for missionaries. We did this about every four years. Have you ever sat in a church service when a missionary was the visiting speaker, with slide shows and pledge cards? That was us. At church, we were treated like heroes. At school, however, I felt like a walking Save the Children commercial—and my teacher wanted to change the channel.

We lived in a two-bedroom trailer in Prairieville, Louisiana. The boys slept in the living room, my parents slept in the middle room, and I shared the back bedroom with extended family, depending on who was in town. While on furlough in America, my mom had my two youngest brothers.

Years later, another furlough sent me back to the United States at a truly awkward time for any girl: middle school. I never seemed to fit in, never felt comfortable in my own skin. I was extremely self-conscious, thinking I was not pretty at all. I thought the American girls my age were so put together, so beautiful, so rich and talented—so much of everything that I wasn't. I made the mistake of comparing myself to them, wanting to look like the girl next door instead of simply *me*. Comparison is poison.

I grew to associate school with humiliation, fear, being at the bottom, always being the foreigner, never belonging. Whenever I walked into a school cafeteria, the memories flooded my emotions; my hands trembled with sweat, my heart thrashed around like a bird caught in a trap, and my lungs felt like they were glued shut. To this day, when I walk into a school cafeteria, I still get nervous—but thankfully, not as badly as in the past.

So why, at age sixteen, did I leave home with a one-way ticket to the United States, where I would have to go to an American school again?

My mother always said, "God doesn't have any grandchildren—just sons and daughters." So, as we each have our own relationship with God, I began to understand that we each have our own call, our own mission. My parents' calling was the interior of the Amazon, teaching locals how to make bricks, dig wells, and farm, eventually making disciples of Christ and planting a church. It was beautiful to behold. Yet, as I deepened my own relationship with Christ, I began to sense that my parents' sacred, God-given assignment wasn't mine. A gentle whisper I couldn't silence kept calling me, wooing me, to the place of my greatest self-doubt and anxiety: the United States.

In addition to following the call of God, I saw moving to America as an opportunity to slay those giants from my past that still haunted me: the fear and failure I had always associated with American schools. So, with all my possessions in a single borrowed suitcase and some cash Dad pulled from his wallet as we said good-bye, I left Manaus for America. As I sat on the plane near the emergency exit, I closed my eyes and daydreamed about what my life would be like. I wasn't naively tilting my head side to side and humming "Someday My Prince Will Come," nor was I plotting how I would become the next immigrant success story. Honestly, all I could think about was finding a church to call home and a church family that would love and accept me. My parents and grandparents had spent their lives seeking out tribes in the Amazon. Now it was time to find my own tribe—in Louisiana.

I chose Louisiana because my aunt (my mother's sister) lived there with her husband. Years earlier, on the furlough during middle school, she had gone with us to America. She met an American, married, and stayed. She was like a sister to me. She and her husband graciously welcomed me into their home, caring for me like I was their own. I even had my own room with all the comforts, including one thing I had never had in Brazil: air conditioning.

My aunt and uncle shared my values about church and church family. They also knew the importance of getting me plugged into a church environment where I would be grounded in faith during my teen years. They knew the impact of a healthy church life. My uncle had heard of a brand-new church that had the reputation for welcoming young people. We got dressed one Sunday morning and took a fifteen-minute drive on Interstate 10 into Baton Rouge. We exited on Highland Road and drove to Healing Place Church (known then as Trinity Christian Center). I remember walking through the front door and immediately feeling the warmth. Friendly smiles greeted me right away. The music was powerful, heavenly. Later, when the senior pastor walked up, introduced himself, and shook our hands, I felt very much at home. What a huge impression this place made on my young heart. I *liked* this place. We left that Sunday morning knowing we had found our new home. We went back Sunday after Sunday. I had a newfound family—plus food every Sunday evening after church. The entire church would head upstairs and eat together. Allow me to be practical here for just a minute; they had *pizza*. In Brazil, pizza was a special treat we had only on rare occasions when in Manaus. This church had it all the time—and it was free! I always looked forward to Sunday evening, especially when it was pizza night. My love for pizza grew each week. I sure enjoyed it at church—and did I mention it was free? I couldn't believe it; free food and acceptance by really nice, loving people. I wanted to be loved and embraced, and I found those needs met there.

My newfound church excelled at showcasing the heart of Jesus through serving, and it kept me going back for more. This was where I wanted and needed to be. I knew that God had brought me here, because Healing Place Church was an answer to my prayers. Everything within me was shouting, "This is your home! Unpack your bags and make yourself comfortable." My heart was settled. I had found my tribe. This church home, this church family, would help cultivate me into the woman I am today.

God answered my prayer to find a place where I could belong and be accepted for who I am. The local church is where I have experienced my deepest relationships, where I have been carried at my weakest, and where I have found hope at my lowest.

You don't grow up in a missionary home without learning the value of work, so finding a job was a top priority. Finding a job was easy; actually getting hired was the hard part. It seemed I didn't have many marketable skills. I didn't even know how to use a phone book. God worked a miracle, however, because I eventually survived an interview and landed the perfect job for me: retail sales in men's clothing.

When you know more about your merchandise than your customers do, you're in a better position to help them make choices—and make a sale. When your customer knows very little, this is quite easy. My typical customer would rush in the store at the same time—3 p.m.—in the same state of mind—desperate—with the same story: "Help! I need a new outfit for a date tonight." I could pick their size the moment they walked into our store. (I guess growing up with four brothers was a marketable skill. Who knew?) I quickly learned to color-coordinate their shirts, pants, suits, and ties like an expert. This experience taught me how to relate to people, discern what they needed, and help meet those needs. Picking out suits and ties might not sound like traditional ministry, but God knew He was preparing me for my future in His kingdom. I enjoyed this first retail experience and enjoyed making some money. After I opened a bank account, my uncle taught me how to write checks and log them into my checkbook. Now that I had a bank account, I was ready to focus on the next thing I wanted to accomplish.

Despite my school experiences—maybe because of them—I wanted to go to college and earn a degree in psychology. But first, I needed to finish high school. Actually, I needed to *start* high school.

Up to this point, I had the American equivalent of a seventh- or eighth-grade education. The prospect of spending the next four years in high school was unacceptable—I was *obsessed* with going to college. I enrolled in a General Equivalency Diploma (GED) program, brushed up on my math (not my favorite), took the test, and... I passed! In my excitement, I applied to Southeastern Louisiana University (SLU), enrolled for classes beginning the fall semester, and then—oops—realized I didn't have transportation to get there.

SLU was in Hammond, about an hour from where I lived in Ascension Parish. So, I did what any problem-solving missionary kid raised in the Amazon would do: I caught rides to school for a few months. I once spent an entire week at the same girl's house because I couldn't get home. But I learned something valuable from her: how to turn on a computer. Well, with the help of my lovely, generous church, I was given a stick shift Chevy Nova. I can't remember the model year, but—trust me—it was old! I learned how to drive it in one weekend and drove it to school for the first time on Tuesday. I didn't even know how to put gas in my little car. Although self-service gas stations are the norm in America, they are rare in Brazil.

Going to college was a leap of faith for me. I had to face those doubts and demons from the past that wanted to hold me back. I remember crying myself to sleep, asking God to please help me with my fear. I feared hallways. I feared teachers. I feared being lost on campus, not finding my way around. I feared being made fun of. I feared failing. After all, I was traumatized by *first grade*. What was I doing here? This was *crazy*.

Just as God helped me in my first weeks at PQQ, He was faithful and helped me again at SLU. By "doing things afraid" and forcing myself to face my fears, I discovered something greater in me: the true source of my faith and courage—and it wasn't willpower. Let me share with you 1 John 4:18 NIV: "There is no fear in love. But perfect love drives out fear, because fear has to do with punishment. The one who fears is not made perfect in love." The Bible is referring to the love God has for us, the love that removed all our sins, the love that moved Jesus to take the punishment for them, the love that promises us eternal life. Since that love has already vanquished our most dangerous enemy, what really remains to be afraid of? God's love casts out—throws away—fear. There's no place for it. It doesn't belong in your life. You don't have to tolerate it. Think of fear as a pebble in your shoe. Now, you can claim that the pebble doesn't hurt while you try not to think about how much it hurts; you can exert willpower over the hurt caused by the pebble and assert that it won't prevent you from walking—and you might even stomp your foot a few times for emphasis; or you could simply throw away the pebble. That's what God's love does with our fear: throws it away. Sometimes, however, the head games caused by the pebble distract us from discernment, and in the fog of the moment, we forget that we really do have authority to remove our shoes and throw the pebbles away. I still have to remind myself of this; it's a recurring battle for me, removing pebbles.

I share my struggles with you, dear reader, because I know how easy it is to glamorize people simply because they are on stage—whether they teach or preach or sing—and I want you to know that those of us in full-time ministry do not lead flawless, perfectly ordered lives, floating from church service to church service, quoting Scripture to one another in Greek and Hebrew. Life isn't always easy, or fair, or safe—no matter who you are; all the more reason to surrender control of our lives to Jesus.

Allow me to share another Scripture, 2 Corinthians 12:7b–10 NIV.

> Therefore, in order to keep me from becoming conceited, I was given a thorn in my flesh, a messenger of Satan, to torment me. Three times I pleaded with the Lord to take it away from me. But he said to me, "My grace is sufficient for you, for my power is made perfect in weakness." Therefore I will boast all the more gladly about my weaknesses, so that Christ's power may rest on me. That is why, for Christ's sake, I delight in weaknesses, in insults, in hardships, in persecutions, in difficulties. For when I am weak, then I am strong.

Not only is it okay to acknowledge our weakness, but it is for our benefit. Whenever we can't, God can. Prideful charades are stressful and exhausting—and people who know you can see through them anyway. Why deprive ourselves of God's grace and power? I would much rather admit my weakness, surrender control to God, and watch Him accomplish what I never could and get all the glory for every success.

Oh—my grades were good, by the way. Not all A's, but good. To God be the glory, definitely.

Meanwhile, by the time I turned seventeen, my days of feeling like a guest at Healing Place Church were long gone. I felt like part of the family. Guests get hospitality; family members get chores. I wanted chores, to do my share. I recognized a need that matched a skill I had: I could take care of kids. So I talked to the overworked nursery leaders and offered my services. "Of course," they said. "You can start now!" *Wow. That was fast.* These girls, like my customers at the clothing store, sounded desperate—and, once again, someone else's desperation created an opportunity for me to help, to serve.

I loved my five years working around spit-up, dirty diapers, and screaming babies. It was in the nursery that I grew from being a volunteer to being a leader, from taking directives to taking ownership. Keeping the nursery clean, the kids safe and happy, and the parents comfortable: they were more than responsibilities; they were my ministry.

It's easy to think of serving God as "out there, somewhere," as if it can only be seen with a spiritual telescope. We expend so much effort trying to figure out God's will for our future that we overlook God's will for our *now*. Open your eyes. Look for a need in front of you, and don't be afraid to volunteer. God will prepare you for what He's planned for you with what's in front of you. So be faithful with today, and trust God with the future.

Allow me to float a couple of stories in your head for a moment.

In Jeremiah 18, God uses a potter making pottery to demonstrate how He shapes and develops us. The potter, with his bare hands, transforms mere clay into a beautiful vessel. But it isn't ready for use until it goes through the fire. How does the potter knows when the vessel is ready? He thumps it. If it sings, it's ready; if it thuds, it goes back into the fire until the next thump.

In Numbers 22, Balaam mistakenly thinks his obstinate donkey is sabotaging his journey—only to discover that God was using it to spare his life. In verse 33, an angel tells Balaam, "The donkey saw me and turned away from me these three times. If it had not turned away, I would certainly have killed you by now."

Here's how these different stories fit this season of my life. For the first time in a long time—after the soul wound of abuse, the anxiety of my school struggles, being a dual citizen yet feeling out of place in both countries, and feeling insecure about my appearance—I was beginning to sing. I was thriving. I was comfortable in my own skin. And then my little donated car began dying on me. Again and again it broke down. All my attempts to attend SLU seemed to be sabotaged. At this point, I began to spiritually reevaluate my situation. Though I had been obsessed with earning a degree, all the "godly sabotage" in my life pointed to leaving school. So I did, and had a peace about it. Why? I see now that SLU was my time back in the fire. Looking back, although I was seeking credentials, I found my confidence. God didn't need my college experience to use me, but He knew that I did. So, although I was supremely focused on college, it was only part of the process; it wasn't the ultimate purpose. Once you can sing when you're thumped, there's no reason to put you back in the fire. You're ready. Please know, dear reader, I was and remain pro-education.

The journey from Manaus to Baton Rouge required huge faith and trust. Leaving one country and culture for another is not an easy transition, but God provided a new home, a new church family, and a newfound confidence birthed in fire. Psalm 37:4 NIV instructs us to "Take delight in the LORD, and he will give you the desires of your heart." When we seek Him, He does just that, in His perfect timing. The church that I longed for on that midnight flight became my new home: the place where I would find my purpose, my husband, and my dream.

More Than I Asked or Imagined

> Though one may be overpowered, two can defend themselves. A cord of three strands is not quickly broken.
>
> —Ecclesiastes 4:12 NIV

At the tender age of eighteen, I wanted to get married. I was determined to be married sometime that calendar year and even made it the focus of my prayers. My future husband, Aley, didn't realize this at the time. I didn't tell him because we weren't dating yet. In fact, we didn't even know each other; it would be another seven years before we met. Although I was obsessed with getting married, it would be accurate to say that I wasn't in what you would call a "serious" dating relationship. It would also be accurate to say that I wasn't in what you would call a "casual" dating relationship. Okay, to be perfectly honest, I didn't have a boyfriend at all. Yet, I was determined to get married—that same year! (Sigh.)

I include this awkward admission because I'm pretty sure I'm not the only one who's ever felt this way. *Um marido* (a husband) was first on my list of dreams I gave my grandmother. The Bible was full of Scriptures that endorse marriage. This *had* to be God's will for my life—so why wasn't it happening?

In my situation, although I prayed for it constantly, I clearly was not ready for marriage, so God did not grant my request. However, our prayer lives need to focus on God's will, not ours; that's why His answers to our petitions can be a variation of *yes, no,* or *wait.* I'm thankful that God is wiser than our prayers. A brief but startling passage in Luke 9:53–56 HCSB illustrates this:

> But they did not welcome Him, because He determined to journey to Jerusalem. When the disciples James and John saw this, they said, "Lord, do You want us to call down fire from heaven to consume them?"
>
> But He turned and rebuked them, and they went to another village.

Yikes! Sincere people—even the disciples—can make some reckless and disturbing requests. Let me say it again: I'm thankful that God is wiser than our prayers. I'm thankful for the times when God says no. He has surely spared me and you from needless heartache by saying no, or simply, "Wait."

So, why does He make us wait?

I don't presume to have every possible answer to this question, but I know of one that applies to a lot of situations:

the timing isn't right. In my situation at age eighteen, I wasn't ready; I was lonely. I had not yet met the man God had chosen for me. I had not yet achieved the closure from the hurt surrounding my abuse. It would be another two years before I finally told someone about it, and my uncle's apology was still a few years in the future. There were other factors, as well. Such as… no boyfriend!

The different plotlines of this part of my life story would eventually intersect at the right time for my good. Timing is important to God. I think of the book of Esther in the Bible. (I encourage you to read this exciting story of God's divine timing and protection.) Esther realized that God composed her real-life fairytale to prevent a genocidal nightmare, that all the strands of her life tied together "for such a time as this," and she courageously seized the moment God orchestrated.

God's timing is perfect. Always.

Regard those dreams that God places in your heart as seeds of hope. Just because they don't sprout right away doesn't mean that the dream died; sometimes the seeds of hope are simply dormant. Seed dormancy, without getting too technical, is all about waiting for the right time to sprout. If the time isn't right, the new growth will die. God knows when the time is right, whether we do or not; God's timing is always perfect. When you leave the timing to God, do you really think He would let His own dream die?

> But when the right time came, God sent his
> Son, born of a woman, subject to the law.
> —Galatians 4:4 NLT

Your eyes saw me when I was formless; all my
days were written in Your book and planned
before a single one of them began.
                        —Psalm 139:16 HCSB

For we are God's masterpiece. He has created
us anew in Christ Jesus, so we can do the
good things he planned for us long ago.
                        —Ephesians 2:10 NLT

God is more than able to write the epic poem—the
masterpiece—that is your life story, including your love story,
and still live eternally outside the pages of your life. He is not
stressed or intimidated by your clock or your calendar; He is
in all ways higher and more infinite than any concept we have
of time. His timing is always perfect, although I didn't grasp
that when I was eighteen.

In hindsight, however, I can see how God lovingly wrote
the different plot points of my life story, arranged the scattered
strands of my love story, and tied them all together at just the
right moment—for my good. Allow me to share a few of these
strands with you.

Strand One: Purity

Have you ever been awake in the middle of the night
when your household is quiet? You hear everything, don't you?
The refrigerator hums; the air conditioner roars; the clock's

incessant ticktocks echo in your eardrums. The slightest sound seems *so loud* at night. Of course, these noises are just as loud in the daytime, but they are drowned out by the even louder noises of everyday life. I'm reminded of the passage in 1 Kings 19:11–12 when God spoke to the prophet Elijah, not in the mighty wind that shattered cliffs, nor in the subsequent earthquake, nor in the following fire, but in a gentle whisper. Not surprisingly, many refer to their daily moments of prayer and Bible reading as *quiet time.*

A spiritual retreat is simply the long version of this process: subtracting noise and distractions in order to devote our full attention to God. As a young teen, I went on such a retreat, and it was an amazing weekend that I shall forever cherish. Part of the experience is simply getting away from our usual surroundings; when you already live in the Amazon Rainforest, the logical choice is to go *deep* into the jungle. In order to reach my girls-only retreat, I took a weeklong boat ride on the Amazon River, winding along its tributaries in a small wooden boat. I slept under the stars each night in a suspended hammock. The sensation of sleeping without anything solid beneath me, combined with the swaying of my hammock and the rocking of the boat, made me feel as though God Himself was holding me in His lap and singing lullabies over me. The river where we traveled was so clean that it was transparent; at times, we seemed to paddle on a liquid mirror.

Our destination was a tiny village tucked deep in the back pocket of nowhere. Avila was a metropolis by comparison. Our amenities were the river, a communal fire pit, and simple wooden huts. This sparse village lacked all the distractions of present-day civilization. Whatever modern conveniences you can think of, we didn't have them. In other words, this was the perfect spot for a spiritual retreat.

By the time I met the elder in charge, bathed in the Amazon River, and ate in front of the fire pit, all the layers insulating me from contemplation had melted away. Both my physical and spiritual senses were—there's no other word for it—*illuminated.* I sat with the other girls on retreat around the fire pit and listened to the elder talk about purity, concluding with: "I challenge you to make a commitment to God that you will remain pure until the night of your wedding. And now ... find a place where you can be alone with your Creator and commit your life to Him, and to purity."

I left the fire pit, grabbed my Bible, and quietly padded toward a spot on the riverbank. I trembled with anticipation, knowing that each step brought me closer to an encounter with the Creator of the universe. I sat on a patch of grass mixed with thistles and shrubs just as the sun was beginning to set. I watched mosquitoes ski on the still water, leaving the faintest creases on its glassy surface. I breathed in the pure, unpolluted air perfumed with the fragrances of fruit trees and wildflowers. I listened to the familiar cries of monkeys and the chorus of hundreds of birds singing the day to sleep. Immersed in this surreal landscape, I felt as if God had created this enchanting place just for me, just for this moment. This was the perfect time and place to make a solemn commitment to the one who created all things. In my spirit, I knew that—as beautiful as this ethereal sunset was—this moment was not about nature, but rather its glorious Creator.

After a few moments of silence, I reaffirmed Christ's lordship over my life, submitting to whatever calling He would place on me. In that moment, I made a vow that I would not even kiss until my wedding day. Though this was a commitment deeper than I could muster in my own strength, I knew there was no turning back. Although I never returned to that tiny village, I never forgot the vow I made there; I never broke it, either.

> Promise me, O women of Jerusalem, not to
> awaken love until the time is right.
> —Song of Songs 8:4 NLT

The purity God requires is not merely physical; it is also mental and emotional. He wants every part of us—including our thought lives—holy and set apart for Him. The choice to remain pure is a daily, intentional decision. I knew the choice was a tough one, but I also knew that whatever God had for me in the future would be awesome. I made a decision to be pure on purpose and put to sleep all of my physical desires until the time was right: my wedding day. Just as I was criticized, judged, and misunderstood at times for choosing the path of purity, you probably will be, too. That's okay. God created you to stand out, not to blend in. Listen to the words of Jesus: "If the world hates you, remember that it hated me first. The world would love you as one of its own if you belonged to it, but you are no longer part of the world. I chose you to come out of the world, so it hates you" (John 15:18-19 NLT).

And here is what the apostle Paul said: "Obviously, I'm not trying to win the approval of people, but of God. If pleasing people were my goal, I would not be Christ's servant" (Galatians 1:10 NLT).

Don't be ashamed of your purity or hide it by not telling others. I believe a lifestyle of purity is part of our relationship with God. We become like the people we spend time with, right? The more you spend time with God, the more you will be like Him.

Day after day, I resolved to stay on the path of purity. I experienced closeness and intimacy—the very things that we girls long for—with the one who loves and accepts me as I am, and who has never violated or abused me.

This topic of purity is dear to me, but giving it the space it deserves would take an entire book, and—God willing—one day I will do that. So, before I move on to the next strand of my love story, I want to emphasize two things.

First, purity is not about preventing pleasure; it's about preventing heartache. God designed us to bond emotionally with our sexual partners; our brains even release hormones for this purpose. The Bible refers to this dynamic throughout Scripture.

> This is why a man leaves his father and mother and bonds with his wife, and they become one flesh.
>
> —Genesis 2:24 HCSB

"Haven't you read," He replied, "that He who created them in the beginning made them male and female," and He also said: 'For this reason a man will leave his father and mother and be joined to his wife, and the two will become one flesh?' So they are no longer two, but one flesh. Therefore, what God has joined together, man must not separate."

—Matthew 19:4–6 HCSB

Don't you realize that your bodies are actually parts of Christ? Should a man take his body, which is part of Christ, and join it to a prostitute? Never! And don't you realize that if a man joins himself to a prostitute, he becomes one body with her? For the Scriptures say, "The two are united into one." But the person who is joined to the Lord is one spirit with him.

Run from sexual sin! No other sin so clearly affects the body as this one does. For sexual immorality is a sin against your own body. Don't you realize that your body is the temple of the Holy Spirit, who lives in you and was given to you by God? You do not belong to yourself, for God bought you with a high price. So you must honor God with your body.

—1 Corinthians 6:16–20 NLT

Since you bond with each sexual partner, can you see how sharing your heart with multiple partners sets you up for emotional conflict and heartbreak? You and your (future) spouse deserve 100 percent of each other's purity.

Second, if you have not walked in purity, today is the day for a fresh start. It is never too late to make a commitment to remain pure. Your sexual history is not greater than the cross of Christ.

> The teachers of the law and the Pharisees brought in a woman caught in adultery. They made her stand before the group and said to Jesus, "Teacher, this woman was caught in the act of adultery. In the Law Moses commanded us to stone such women. Now what do you say?" They were using this question as a trap, in order to have a basis for accusing him.
>
> But Jesus bent down and started to write on the ground with his finger. When they kept on questioning him, he straightened up and said to them, "Let any one of you who is without sin be the first to throw a stone at her." Again he stooped down and wrote on the ground.
>
> At this, those who heard began to go away one at a time, the older ones first, until only Jesus was left, with the woman still standing there. Jesus straightened up and

asked her, "Woman, where are they? Has no one condemned you?"

"No one, sir," she said.

"Then neither do I condemn you," Jesus declared. "Go now and leave your life of sin."

—John 8:3–11 NIV

Notice the two things Jesus told the woman in verse 11: "neither do I condemn you" and "Go now and leave your life of sin." Isn't that beautiful? Jesus rescues you where you are and loves you enough to say, "Go now and leave your life of sin."

God is calling you to that secret place where you make your solemn vow to Him. You don't have to go on a retreat like I did. You can do it right now, while you're reading this book. My prayer for you is that you commit to a lifestyle of purity. You will not regret it; neither will your spouse.

Strand Two: Happily Single

Above all else, guard your heart, for everything you do flows from it.

—Proverbs 4:23 NIV

Contrary to what you hear in fairy tales and love songs, unhappiness is a terrible reason to get married. It's ironic that many unhappy singles believe they would be happy if only they were married, because many unhappy marrieds believe they would be happy if only they were single. Whether you're single or married, it's a tragic blunder to give another human being the responsibility (and power) to make you either happy or unhappy. It's not only an emotional mistake but also a spiritual one. You can't promote another person to number one in your life without demoting God. God has to be first— period. If we don't get our relationship with God right, it's easy to get our relationships with people wrong—especially the romantic ones.

If you feel like you'll never be happy until you're married, or until you're a parent, or until you're rich, or until you lose ten pounds, or until… whatever, you'll *never* be happy. Why? You can't chase happiness without running away from joy. Happiness is a fleeting emotion; it comes and goes with the circumstances of life. Joy comes from the presence of God (Psalm 16:11) and the Holy Spirit (Galatians 5:22). If you remain in the presence of God and nurture your relationship with Him through His Son Jesus Christ (John 15:5), you will have joy and contentment that no life circumstance can take away.

Here are the words of Jesus, using a vineyard to describe our relationship with Him: "I am the vine; you are the branches. The one who remains in Me and I in him produces much fruit, because you can do nothing without Me" (John 15:5 HCSB).

And here is the the fruit you will produce if you simply remain in (relationship with) Jesus: "But the Holy Spirit produces this kind of fruit in our lives: love, joy, peace, patience, kindness, goodness, faithfulness, gentleness, and self-control. There is no law against these things!" (Galatians 5:22–23 NLT)

So we grow and produce the spiritual fruit listed above—including joy—simply by staying in relationship with Jesus, like branches stay connected to a tree. Jesus said we can do nothing without Him. Makes sense; I've never seen firewood bloom.

> I know both how to have a little, and I know how to have a lot. In any and all circumstances I have learned the secret of being content—whether well fed or hungry, whether in abundance or in need. I am able to do all things through Him who strengthens me. Still, you did well by sharing with me in my hardship.
>
> —Philippians 4:12–14 HCSB

The secret of being content in all circumstances is recognizing that the source of all we need in life—including love and joy—is God. We all have a God-shaped void in our lives that only He can fill. Nothing else fits; no one else satisfies. We can do nothing without Jesus (John 15:5), but we can do all things through Him (Philippians 4:13). Jesus wants to be Lord—the boss—of your entire life, including your love life. In light of the truth of these Scriptures, making Jesus the Lord of your love life is one of the wisest decisions you will ever make.

Dear friends, let us continue to love one another, for love comes from God. Anyone who loves is a child of God and knows God. But anyone who does not love does not know God, for God is love.

God showed how much he loved us by sending his one and only Son into the world so that we might have eternal life through him. This is real love—not that we loved God, but that he loved us and sent his Son as a sacrifice to take away our sins.

Dear friends, since God loved us that much, we surely ought to love each other.

—1 John 4:7–11 NLT

Real love begins and ends with God, and the secret to a fruitful marriage is having God at the root of it. So, don't give your heart away just because you're lonely or unhappy; focus on your relationship with God. Stay connected to Christ and keep your focus on Him, following wherever He leads. At just the right time, your journey will intersect with God's best for you.

When you do find someone, don't date like you're married. Date like you're single: keep pure and guard your heart. And once you're married, you can stop acting like you're single: enjoy being one flesh with the love God chose for you.

Strand Three: My Husband

In the early days of Healing Place Church, before the arena was built, finding a seat was difficult. If you didn't arrive early, you could end up stuck in the foyer. Our congregation would stream into the sanctuary like shoppers storming a department store on Black Friday. One Sunday, I was so focused on getting a seat that I didn't notice a certain young man until I slammed into him. I muttered a quick "I'm sorry" and kept moving. (Remember, I was *focused* on getting a seat.) I had no idea that the handsome stranger I had nearly trampled was my future husband: Aley Demarest.

At the time, I was on a self-imposed relationship sabbatical. I was previously engaged, and I had painfully learned that matters of the heart are never casual.

> The heart is deceitful above all things and
> beyond cure. Who can understand it?
> —Jeremiah 17:9 NIV

In my heart, I felt that a certain young man was *the one.* Yet, I didn't have peace in my spirit, only a heavy burden. Stress and uncertainty make a poor foundation for a lifelong relationship. So, I prayed. I lamented. I cried. I vented. Why was I feeling this? How could I possibly make the wrong choice? Even after I prayed about it? I finally quieted down, dropped my defenses, and just listened. In a still, small voice, the Holy Spirit said, "I want you to let him go."

Wow. *Wow.* I had a choice: follow my heart or obey God. It wasn't easy, but I chose to obey God. The next day, I very nicely tried to explain to my suitor what had happened. The whole "God told me to break up with you" story didn't go as smoothly as I had hoped. I hurt him deeply, and hurting him hurt me deeply. I never wanted to hurt anyone like that again. Because of that heartache, I wanted my next relationship to be my last, to be my soulmate, to be the love of my life: *meu marido* (my husband). So I took a break from dating altogether—a sabbatical—to help me heal emotionally, get a fresh perspective on my life choices, and complete the transition from being a teenager obsessed with marriage to being a child whose first love is her heavenly Father. I learned to trust that, when the time was right, God would send *the one* who would run the spiritual marathon of life alongside me. Still, I had no clue that God had placed Aley and me on a *literal* collision course.

A few months after we, um, first bumped into each other, Aley attended a class I was teaching. He thought my twin Edwin and I were a couple. Edwin, addressing the entire class, shattered this illusion with "Does anyone want to date my sister? Because she's single."

Soon after that awkward moment, on a rainy Wednesday night as I was leaving church, Edwin told me that someone wanted to meet me. I nodded and followed him straight to Aley. I can still remember our handshake. I liked the firm grip, and my heart skipped a beat. When our eyes locked, I could feel his passion and attraction for me. Electricity seemed to flow from his hand into mine all the way to my heart. Everything within me wanted to fall into his arms right then and express all that I was feeling inside, including my attraction for him. (Of course, I didn't. Remember, girls, falling into a guy's arms and expressing your undying love after an introductory handshake is *always* a bad idea.)

After he excused himself, I just stood there, dumbstruck. I had so many thoughts and emotions charging through me that I couldn't process them all. I was thinking I should be cautious, yet I couldn't take my eyes off of him as he walked away. I was a mess—and after only a *handshake*.

After I composed myself, I decided to leave. Aley was walking out the door as I approached the exit. We started talking, and time stood still. Aley walked me to my car, but I didn't get in; we kept talking. It began to rain; we kept talking. We both got drenched; we kept talking.

Aley called that same week, asking me out to lunch. I flatly refused. I didn't want to end my relationship sabbatical—even go on a single date—unless I was sure Aley could be the one. I had started praying the night we met, seeking God's will over whether to pursue a relationship. I had felt peace, but the Bible says, "Every fact is to be confirmed by the testimony of two or three witnesses" (2 Corinthians 13:1b NASB). So I called my parents in Brazil. I told them I was quickly falling in love and asked them to pray, too. I wanted them to somehow hear from God that this was Mr. Right. I also asked my brothers and closest friends to pray. Within twenty-four hours, my parents called back and told me to give this potential relationship a shot; they would continue to pray.

The relationship sabbatical was over!

Deep inside, I had peace that Aley was the one. That peace was there from the beginning and never left. Still, I kept on praying, seeking God, and maintaining accountability.

I got to know Aley on a friendship level, and our relationship blossomed. We grew fonder of each other by the minute. At the very beginning of our relationship, I had to break the news to Aley that I had made a vow that I would not so much as kiss until my wedding day. His response (to my surprise) was, "Great. That's awesome. I will respect your wish." I was so relieved; it made me love him even more. I could hardly wait to see him before each date, which we went on as often as possible. When we couldn't be together, we spent countless hours on the phone.

The more time we spent together, the more I saw and experienced the gentleman side of him. I loved that he opened my car door and the doors to restaurants, always treating me like a princess. I knew that I could give him my heart, and it would not be crushed. Aley was more than I could have ever prayed for.

> Delight yourself in the LORD; and He will
> give you the desires of your heart.
> —Psalm 37:4 NASB

Our relationship progressed quickly. Three months after our first date, we were engaged. Three months after that, we were married. Since it would be impossible for the entire family in Brazil to attend our Baton Rouge wedding, we planned an engagement ceremony in Brazil just for them.

The ceremony was scheduled to start at seven p.m., which meant that everyone showed up closer to nine. (The perception of time and the concept of punctuality are very different in Brazil.) My father made sure everything was ready, then walked me in on a red runner. With every step, my heart beat faster. Two native violinists played my favorite love songs. Tables were draped in white satin accented with my favorite color: dark red. Exotic flowers were everywhere. Although the room was beautiful, I really wanted to look into the eyes of my beloved. Sparks flew when our eyes finally met. For a brief moment, only Aley and I existed; the rest of the world faded away. Aley wore a white linen shirt that complemented my beautiful white gown. As I turned to face our audience, Aley dropped to one knee and presented a wooden box with an engagement ring fit for a princess. I couldn't take my eyes off of it, sparkling and custom-made just for me. Aley whispered, "Will you be my wife?" and slipped the ring on my finger. I joyfully nodded yes! Everyone celebrated our engagement late into the night; then the family prayed over us and blessed our upcoming marriage.

Later, on our wedding day, when Aley and I kissed for the first time, I felt like God smiled on us. All those years, I had kept my vow. I had remained pure. God honored that commitment by blessing me with a godly man, a true gentleman, and a smart, caring provider: Albert Aloysius Demarest III.

> Trust in the LORD with all your heart; do not
> depend on your own understanding. Seek his

will in all you do, and he will show you which
path to take.

—Proverbs 3:5–6 NLT

If you honor God in all you do, why wouldn't He bless you? We cannot even fathom the amazing plans that God has for our lives. He wants to reveal His plans to you; so, spend time with Him so you can recognize His voice.

Even in my love story, I realize that God's vision and plans for me surpassed my wildest dreams. There were details about my spouse that I had prayed for and forgotten about, but God didn't. There were desires in my heart that I did not ask of God, yet He provided. Aley possessed qualities that I didn't even realize I needed in a spouse, but God knew. Even now, after years of marriage and three children, I need only look at Aley to be reminded that—because He so perfectly knows and loves us—God's answers far exceed our prayers. Remember, you can always trust His heart and His timing, especially when you can't trust your own.

Now to him who is able to do immeasurably
more than all we ask or imagine, according
to his power that is at work within us, to him
be glory in the church and in Christ Jesus
throughout all generations, for ever and ever!
Amen.

—Ephesians 3:20–21 NIV

Unstoppable Dreams

Before we continue, I want to change up our focus a little. So far, this book has followed my life from South America to the American South, from the Amazon Rainforest to the concrete jungle. I've shared how God shaped me through life experiences, including profound hurts and challenges, and how He was always with me. So, although this book is filled with stories about me, it's not about me at all; it's about God's work in me. My dreams were ultimately from Him. This is not a self-help book; too many of those are just variations of "be like me." This, on the other hand, is a God-help book; my aim all along has been to point you to Jesus. I don't want you to be like me; I want you to *be like Jesus*. In this chapter, I want to underscore that point by taking the focus off of me entirely. Consider this chapter my personal letter to you, dear reader. As you read this, especially the Scriptures, think about the dreams that God has placed in your heart.

Shall we begin?

What do the Panama Canal, the Hoover Dam, and the Roman Pantheon all have in common? They're all really old (the Pantheon was finished in AD 126), and they're all made of concrete. We build roads, bridges, and skyscrapers with concrete because it is durable and strong and gets stronger over time. Anyone who's ever scraped a knee or bumped his or her head on concrete knows how hard and unyielding this man-made invention can be.

Sometimes we feel like our dreams have been buried in concrete. We feel helpless, trapped, and controlled by forces stronger than us.

A teenager I'll call JJ felt like this. JJ had dreams—real, God-given dreams—but also had problems at home. He never really fit in. He had a lot of older siblings that he didn't get along with. Like a lot of kids, JJ tattled on the older children when they slacked on chores. His siblings regarded him as a spoiled, delusional brat. Maybe he was; maybe he wasn't, but what they hated most about him was that he was their father's favorite. Their dad even purchased nicer clothes for JJ than for the others. If JJ had gone to my school in Humaitá, he would have been beaten up and crammed into a locker on a regular basis. Of course, he likely would have been the teacher's pet—and tattled.

All siblings fight, but JJ's relationship with his brothers deteriorated so much that they couldn't speak to him without being hostile. It seemed that JJ's greatest talent was making enemies.

One day, when circumstances placed them all together far from home, far from any intervention from their father, things turned violent. JJ was attacked and stripped by his brothers and then thrown into an old well. Luckily for JJ, the cistern was dry, or he would have drowned. Unluckily for JJ, the cistern was dry, and the fall hurt. Wet or dry, he couldn't climb out. He could only catch his breath and spit out bloody bits of dirt. Once he realized his pleas for help were a waste of energy, he grew quiet. He had plenty of time to think about what was crawling around in the dark with him. In the velvet silence, he heard his brothers up above. And what were they doing? Enjoying a leisurely meal while they brainstormed about how to solve the JJ problem.

Can you imagine listening to your own flesh and blood plot your death? JJ did.

First, they were going to leave him in the cistern to die, but decided against it. After all, some passerby might stumble upon the scene and rescue him. So, they had to kill him sooner rather than later. But *who* would do it? And *how* would they do it? And what would they do with the body? And most importantly: how could they kill their little brother and not get caught? This was sinister, scary, and not going to end well.

Brainstorming became debate; debate grew into argument; argument drifted toward stalemate. Their frustration quickly turned into elation, however, when a solution none of them had thought of passed by—and the JJ problem was solved.

Overwhelmed and discouraged, JJ almost believed the nightmare was over when they finally pulled him out of the cistern. Of course, it wasn't. After all, JJ was a tattletale, a snitch; there was no chance that his brothers would let him go. Imagine the shock and numb awareness he must have felt when he realized they were *selling* him as a slave. They would get rid of JJ, avoid the logistical problem of disposing of the body and the risk of being charged with murder, and make some money, too.

You probably recognize that the JJ I'm talking about is actually Joseph from the Bible. His remarkable story begins in Genesis 37, picks back up in Genesis 39, and continues all the way to Genesis 50. It's one of the most fascinating stories of the Bible, and I encourage you to read it, although it's too long to include here.

What I want to emphasize are the obstacles he faced. He was mocked and persecuted after naively sharing his dreams with people who already hated him. He was sold as a slave to a passing caravan and re-sold in Egypt, a foreign country, with an unfamiliar culture and language. Next, he was falsely accused of sexual assault and imprisoned. His only ally, after being released from prison, forgot him. That overconfident teenager with dreams of grandeur was now pushing thirty, a slave, and in prison with no realistic expectation of freedom. Those dreams he had as a teenager were buried deep under a lifetime of concrete. Opportunities, freedom, *years:* all lost.

But...

> The LORD was with Joseph, and he became a
> successful man, serving in the household of
> his Egyptian master.
> —Genesis 39:2 HCSB

> But the LORD was with Joseph and extended
> kindness to him. He granted him favor in the
> eyes of the prison warden.
>
> —Genesis 39:21 HCSB

Joseph was never alone because God was with him—even in the worst of circumstances. The Bible says that God even extended him kindness and favor. After that day in the cistern, Joseph's life was as hard as concrete, no question. But God planted dreams in him that were stronger than any man-made obstacle. Your dreams are, too.

Let me show you.

Although I grew up in Brazil, I live in South Louisiana now, and this place is full of massive trees. There's this one tree, about an hour from my house, called the Seven Sisters Oak. This southern live oak is about *1500 years old*. Its trunk's circumference is over 38 feet, and its canopy is almost 140 feet across. And it's still growing, even after a near-direct hit from Hurricane Katrina in 2005.

Healing Place Church has a Dream Center campus in North Baton Rouge, and the neighborhoods around it are full of beautiful old oak trees. They aren't as big as the Seven Sisters Oak, but they're still huge. These trees line the streets, forming gorgeous canopies that in some places completely shade the street from one side to the other.

These majestic trees, however, absolutely wreck the sidewalks. Their roots push through solid concrete, breaking it into slabs the size of tabletops. It's amazing, looking at a piece of concrete large enough to crush a grown man, teetering on a single tree root. Talk about quiet strength! The man-made concrete is no match for the trees that God made, trees that were once weak little saplings, trees that were once tiny seeds waiting to sprout.

Just like your dreams.

Now let's get back to Joseph and skip ahead a bit. After prison. After interpreting Pharaoh's dreams. After saving Egypt. After *ruling* Egypt. After getting married and having kids.

> Before the years of famine came, two sons were born to Joseph by Asenath daughter of Potiphera, priest of On. Joseph named his firstborn Manasseh and said, "It is because God has made me forget all my trouble and all my father's household." The second son he named Ephraim and said, "It is because God has made me fruitful in the land of my suffering."
>
> —Genesis 41:50–52 NIV

In the ancient world, names were used to commemorate, to symbolize, to convey something profound. For Joseph, the birth of Manasseh was a moment of such exquisite joy that all the pain of his past blurred into the background, blissfully out of focus. Manasseh means *makes to forget*. Finally, Joseph was free on the inside, too.

A second child was born. He was named Ephraim—*double fruit*—because God had made Joseph fruitful in the land of his suffering; again, a name rich with meaning. Joseph had come to Egypt against his will as a slave. Although innocent, he had spent much of (and possibly all) his adult life in a prison in the ancient world. It was no exaggeration to say that he had suffered. Yet, in the span of a single day, he went from prisoner to prime minister; he was second only to Pharaoh. It must have seemed like, well, a dream. It makes perfect sense that Joseph thought of his life in this progression: suffering, freedom, fruitfulness.

Let's skip ahead again, to Genesis 48. Egypt enjoyed seven amazing years of one bumper crop after another. And since God used Joseph to show them that seven years of famine were coming, Egypt was ready. They had so much food that they had enough to sell to neighboring countries. Guess who showed up to buy grain in Egypt? Joseph's brothers. To make a long story short, Joseph was used by God to save that dysfunctional family of his and bring them to Egypt. They were reunited and reconciled, and Joseph's father (Jacob) was about to die. As was the custom, Joseph wanted his father to bless his two sons. The following is a lengthy passage, but I'm including it for a reason.

> Then Jacob looked over at the two boys. "Are these your sons?" he asked.
>
> "Yes," Joseph told him, "these are the sons God has given me here in Egypt."

And Jacob said, "Bring them closer to me, so I can bless them."

Jacob was half-blind because of his age and could hardly see. So Joseph brought the boys close to him, and Jacob kissed and embraced them. Then Jacob said to Joseph, "I never thought I would see your face again, but now God has let me see your children, too!"

Joseph moved the boys, who were at their grandfather's knees, and he bowed with his face to the ground. Then he positioned the boys in front of Jacob. With his right hand he directed Ephraim toward Jacob's left hand, and with his left hand he put Manasseh at Jacob's right hand. But Jacob crossed his arms as he reached out to lay his hands on the boys' heads. He put his right hand on the head of Ephraim, though he was the younger boy, and his left hand on the head of Manasseh, though he was the firstborn. Then he blessed Joseph and said,

"May the God before whom my grandfather Abraham and my father, Isaac, walked—the God who has been my shepherd all my life, to this very day, the Angel who has redeemed me from all harm—may he bless these boys. May they preserve my name and the names of Abraham and Isaac.

And may their descendants multiply greatly throughout the earth."

But Joseph was upset when he saw that his father placed his right hand on Ephraim's head. So Joseph lifted it to move it from Ephraim's head to Manasseh's head. "No, my father," he said. "This one is the firstborn. Put your right hand on his head."

But his father refused. "I know, my son; I know," he replied. "Manasseh will also become a great people, but his younger brother will become even greater. And his descendants will become a multitude of nations."

So Jacob blessed the boys that day with this blessing: "The people of Israel will use your names when they give a blessing. They will say, 'May God make you as prosperous as Ephraim and Manasseh.'" In this way, Jacob put Ephraim ahead of Manasseh.

—Genesis 48:8–20 NLT

Do you see what Jacob did? He rewrote Joseph's story. Joseph thought that the three acts of his life story were suffering, freedom, and fruitfulness. He thought freedom came before fruitfulness. But Jacob corrected him; he put Ephraim ahead of Manasseh: fruitfulness before freedom.

So often—just like Joseph—we think, "If I can just get that lucky break—get a scholarship, or get married, or get my spouse saved, or have a baby, or get out of debt, or get a better job, or... *whatever,* once life is easy—easy?—*then* I can be fruitful. *Then* I can really serve God. *Then* I'll read my Bible. *Then* I'll pray more. *Then* I'll connect with my local church." *Then, then, then.*

Wrong, wrong, wrong. Lies, lies, lies! I hope this doesn't make you angry, but if it does, that's okay. Be angry, but keep reading because this will help you. Joseph got mad at Jacob in verse 17 and even tried to switch his hands back. Are you going to get mad at God? You may want to say, "No, You don't understand. I'm a victim. I've got a past. I've got issues. I've done time. I've had an abortion. I was sober before and blew it, and I'm scared I might again. I belong on daytime talk TV. You can't use me! I'm not perfect!" Go ahead and try to switch God's hands. Be sure to get a good grip first.

Why not simply let your heavenly Father rewrite your story? The path to freedom is fruitfulness. The way out of your problems is to keep growing. Whether or not your problems stay the same, you will outgrow them.

Human-made obstacles are no match for God-made growth. Remember the trees I talked about earlier that broke right through the concrete and demolished it? When those trees were planted, they were no match for the concrete. Now the concrete is no match for the trees. No one had to bust up the concrete to make room for those trees. They just grew and pushed the concrete out of the way as needed. Is there still concrete in the lives of those trees? Yes. Will there always be? Maybe. But is concrete a legitimate obstacle to any tree that keeps growing? Not at all. The concrete is no longer an issue; it's just a prop to show off how strong the tree is.

It's the same with your life, your issues, your past, your dreams. No one has a problem-free life. We've all got a little concrete in our way. Will it always be there? Maybe. Will it keep you trapped? No; just keep growing. You *will* outgrow your problems. God's plan for you is not to take away your problems so that life will be easy; it's to empower you to break through them—and demonstrate that the same power that raised Christ from the dead is alive in you (see Ephesians 1:19–20). Like concrete teetering on a tree root, your problems are just evidence for your testimony, to show off how strong God is in you.

Joseph was seventeen when God gave him very specific dreams. They didn't come to pass until he was about thirty-seven. When Joseph was seventeen, he wasn't ready; he was no match for the concrete. But he grew a lot in twenty years. Joseph's "breakthrough moment" was decades in the making, as it was for those oak trees in North Baton Rouge, as it was for me, as it might be for you. If you grow weary in the waiting, remember to trust God's timing. The longer the wait, the bigger the breakthrough. So the next time you see a tree busting up a sidewalk, let that remind you to "just keep growing." The path to freedom is fruitfulness. The way out of your problems is to keep growing.

My prayer for you is that you would do these things:

1. Confess Jesus Christ as your Lord and Savior, and daily nurture your relationship with Him as the most important part of your life.
2. Know that your heavenly Father loves and treasures you and has a plan and a purpose for your life, and that it is good.
3. Feel secure enough in His love to trust Him not only with your eternity, but with your moments and decisions.
4. Embrace the story God has written for you. Courageously seize the moments God has planned for you. Dare to dream.

Postscript

Hope deferred makes the heart sick, but a dream fulfilled is a tree of life.

—Proverbs 13:12 NLT

Remember this list from Chapter One?

- *um marido*
- *um emprego*
- *um carro*
- *vitória*
- *sabedoria*
- *inteligência*
- *escrever um livro*

They've all come true.

A few years ago, Grandma revealed that she kept this list tucked in her Bible for nearly twenty years, praying those seven dreams over my life. Oh, the faith of a grandmother! I now carry it in my wallet as a reminder that God is faithful to the dreams He plants in our hearts. What began as a childhood list of wishes is now a testimony that all things are possible with God. Grandma taught me the power of praying your dreams into existence, no matter how long it takes.

> For nothing is impossible with God.
> — Luke 1:37 NIV

Thank you for allowing me to share my story with you. I would love to hear from you, especially if this book has helped you in some way. You can reach me at AmazonGirlBook@gmail.com. Thanks again, and God bless you.

—Elizabeth